The Intensive Interaction Handbook

The Intensive Interaction Handbook

Dave Hewett, Graham Firth,
Mark Barber and Tandy Harrison

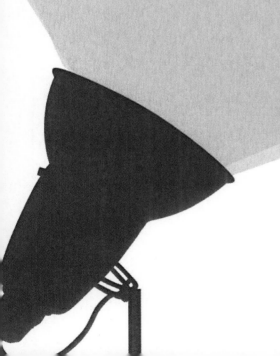

Los Angeles | London | New Delhi
Singapore | Washington DC

First published 2012
Reprinted 2012

SAGE Publications Ltd
1 Oliver's Yard
55 City Road
London EC1Y 1SP

SAGE Publications Inc.
2455 Teller Road
Thousand Oaks, California 91320

SAGE Publications India Pvt Ltd
B 1/I 1 Mohan Cooperative Industrial Area
Mathura Road
New Delhi 110 044

SAGE Publications Asia-Pacific Pte Ltd
3 Church Street
10-04 Samsung Hub
Singapore 049483

Library of Congress Control Number: 2011924955

British Library Cataloguing in Publication data

A catalogue record for this book is available from the British Library

ISBN 978-0-85702-490-9
ISBN 978-0-85702-491-6

Typeset by C&M Digitals (P) Ltd, Chennai, India
Printed and bound by CPI Group (UK) Ltd, Croydon, CR0 4YY
Printed on paper from sustainable resources

Contents

List of figures

About the authors

Dave Hewett has been working in the field of special education for 35 years. He was headteacher at Harperbury Hospital School throughout the 1980s, where the team worked on the development and first research on Intensive Interaction. With Melanie Nind he produced the first Intensive Interaction book in 1994. Since 1990 he has been an independent consultant, continuing to publish and work on the development and dissemination of the approach. He is now director of the Intensive Interaction Institute, broadcasting Intensive Interaction increasingly worldwide.

Graham Firth is Intensive Interaction Project Leader for the Leeds Partnerships NHS Trust. In the 1980s Graham worked for six years as a care assistant at a large residential hospital for adults with learning disabilities in Leeds (UK), before leaving to pursue a career in teaching. Initially spending several years working in primary schools, Graham then went on to teach adults with severe or profound learning disabilities. After becoming dissatisfied with the then asocial pedagogy, he started to work more interactively before formally adopting Intensive Interaction as his main teaching strategy. In 2003 he joined the Leeds Partnerships NHS Trust, where he now works to support others to adopt, sustain and develop their Intensive Interaction practices or services. He is currently the editor of the *UK Intensive Interaction Newsletter* and the Leeds Partnership NHS Trust – Intensive Interaction Webpage (at www.leedspft.nhs.uk), and is a member of the Trust's Severe Challenging Behaviour Team.

Mark Barber worked in the UK as a special educator for 20 years before moving to Australia, where he has introduced Intensive Interaction to over 90 schools and services for learners with severe-profound intellectual disabilities. Mark currently divides his time between working as Intensive Interaction Coordinator and Leading Teacher at Bayside Special Developmental School in Melbourne and working as a Consultant in Profound Intellectual Disability, providing training and support to schools and practitioners in a variety of settings. He coordinates Intensive Interaction across Australia and New Zealand.

Tandy Harrison qualified as a teacher at the University of Cambridge Faculty of Education and developed her interest in play, interaction and learning disability while teaching at Colleges Nursery School in Cambridge. She has two children, George and Lucy. She works as a freelance consultant and became an Intensive Interaction Coordinator two years ago.

Acknowledgements

Thank you first and always to all the wonderful, dedicated, hard-pressed practitioners I have met and worked with over all these years.

Particularly, all those on the Intensive Interaction coordinator courses who give one's brain such a thorough workout.

Thank you especially to the parents who make us practitioners feel humble.

Gratitude and fond memories as ever, to Melanie Nind, for all the years of working and thinking together. Similarly, the staff and students of Harperbury Hospital School with whom we both worked, 1981–1990.

Sarah Forde runs the Intensive Interaction office and gets to do all of the important, detailed, systematic, painstaking background work that ensures us practitioners can do what we do without needing to add up columns of figures.

Thank you to Jacqui Clark for the original artwork.

Alex Molineux and Jude Bowen at SAGE have been the support that writers need publishers to be.

Then variously and in no particular order:

John Carpenter, Jan Gordon, Cath Irvine, Helen Janes, Carol Jones, Jacci Kellett, Uwe Kerat, Penny Lacey, Miranda-Jane McCormick, Lynette Menzies, Julia Rhodes, Ben Smith, Emily Seyler, Lydia Swinton, Mary Turner, Yiannis Vogindroukas, Janee Williamson, Ellen Winter.

Dave Hewett
Malvern

Part 1

Human communication and the background to Intensive Interaction

1

The nature of human communication

Dave Hewett

> **This chapter looks at:**
>
> - **How we communicate**
> - **How communication issues affect all of us.**

Is it not wonderful to be a communicator? Do you not think that human communication is a brilliant thing to take part in, or to watch other people doing? Do you like 'people watching'? Most of us find watching other people's communications to be fascinating don't we?

Think about all the things you do in life that you enjoy. Yes, there are many. But is it not true that the best thing for nearly all of us is just being with other people and chit-chatting? Most of us do plenty of it, every day.

This is a brief introductory chapter about communication in general. Before thinking specifically about communication issues for some people with special communication needs, let us spend a little time thinking about communication issues that affect all of us.

We human beings communicate in a rich and sophisticated way that sets us apart from all other species on our planet. No other animals can communicate like we can. Human beings communicate with incredible detail using language, but we are also probably more detailed *visual* communicators than other animals.

You will often see the phrase 'communication channels', being used. We will use it from time to time in this book; it is useful. Humankind communicates through these channels:

Communication is first and foremost enjoyable

Eye contacts, facial expressions, body language and gesture are as important as speech

Sound. Speech and language, vocalisations such as grunts, then a range of other noises can be communicative – lip-smacking, clapping hands, foot-tapping, and so on.

Vision. Reading each others' signals – facial expressions, eye contacts, gesture, body language, uncontrolled non-conscious visual information coming out of a person.

Most human communications are enjoyable 'chit-chat', but in all communications we visually 'read' each other minutely

Touch, physical contact. Handshakes, hugs, strokes, pats, taps, kissing, caressing, intimate skin to skin contact, and so on.

Smell. We do pick up *olfactory* information from one another, for example, from pheremones, usually on a non-conscious level. We *are* mammals.

Of course, it is the development of language that is the most obvious difference between us and other animals. As said, we can communicate with language in very detailed ways – mostly with speech, but sign language users demonstrate similar complexity and detail.

In fact, all of us who are not sign language users, nonetheless exchange a great deal of visual information, indeed some visual language. During interactions we are watching each other minutely to pick up visual information from the other person(s). This information will be within their:

- facial expressions

- eye contacts and adjustments in eye contact (much of it non-conscious)

- body language and posture (both deliberate and non-conscious)

- gesture (both deliberate and non-conscious)

- proximity and presence and the way in which people physically orientate to each other.

In fact, the scientists who study these things will usually make the observation that human communication is visual communication first and foremost. They will estimate that our communications are around 90 per cent visual. The speech therefore, accounts for the other 8–10 per cent. The speech sort of puts on the 'gloss' of detailed meanings to the communication.

You will notice that in the list above, the phrase 'non-conscious' is used. In studies on human communication, there is increasing awareness of how wonderful our abilities are within face-to-face communication. Try to think for a moment about the process you are experiencing when having a conversation.

During conversation, there is turn-taking with speech of course. But in order to synchronise that turn-taking and be 'in harmony' with each other, it is necessary to 'cue' each other with visual signals and 'tune-in' and read those signals successfully. Otherwise, the conversation is a mess.

More than that, people communicating achieve a sort of psychological and emotional 'tuned-inness' with each other. Each person scans the other person's face minutely second by second in order to pick up tiny bits of visual information that lets you know some general understandings about what the other person is thinking and feeling. You are listening to them with your ears, but also 'listening' with your eyes.

The quality of the eye contact is crucial (we usually find it uncomfortable not to receive any). However, it is also crucial not to make eye contact for too long (extended, rigid eye contact is usually interpreted as a signal of likely aggression by mammals). In British culture, eye contact during conversation is usually in bursts of a few seconds, with eyes moving away and coming back. However, if one person is making a prolonged speech, it can be acceptable to look at them in a sustained way.

This ability to visually 'read' each other takes place at high speed. Some of it, but only a little, is a conscious operation. Most of it is dealt with by cognitions at a non-conscious level – the brain's processing power for this large quantity of information seems to operate better non-consciously. Conclusions from the information are then rapidly fed back into one's consciousness as what feels like intuitive insights into the other person's state of being. This has been called 'automatic cognitive processes'. If you've never thought about this before, human communication turns out to be even more complicated than you thought, does it not?

However, all this probably provides one explanation for why we all like people watching so much. Since we are so visually expert, we can effortlessly pick up interesting titbits of information from people, just by looking at them.

The extent to which people use physical contact communication varies according to a range of factors. An important factor is the nature of the relationship and how well the people know each other. Another factor is culture. There are many studies that observe the differences in physical contact communication between people of different cultures. We must all have personal experiences of this. It is generally observed that traditional, white British society is one where touch communication is not used so frequently or intensively as in many other cultures and countries. These issues are described and analysed in the books by Argyle, Montagu and Field (see Further reading).

However, we all know that plenty of beautiful, warm, physical contact is absolutely critical to the development and well-being of babies. In fact, that seems to be the case for people at early levels of development of whatever age – communication and relationship with touch is extremely important to them. Use of physical contact within interaction is a theme of this book. Intensive Interaction activities can positively employ this channel. The sense in which physical contact issues may be seen as a 'difficulty' in our work is discussed in Chapter 10.

But, back to spoken language. Speech communication is, of course, incredibly important. It has enabled humankind to be different, to do things in complex ways. With speech and language we can talk, write books, have a society, culture, history, government, education, the European Union (EU), the United Nations (UN), the World Bank, cities, cars, space rockets and so on.

But, there is some thinking that the ability for doing these things is not really the purpose nor the main function of human communication. Communication is seen as satisfying all these needs (from Adler and Rodman, 2006):

Physical needs

'Communication is so important that it is necessary for physical health. In fact, evidence suggests that an absence of satisfying communications can even jeopardize life itself ... personal communication is essential for our well-being.'

Identity needs

'Communication does more than enable us to survive. It is the way, indeed the *only* way – we learn who we are ... our sense of identity comes from the way we interact with other people.'

Social needs

These include 'pleasure', 'affection', 'inclusion', 'escape', 'relaxation' and 'control'. Furthermore, 'imagine how empty your life would be if these needs weren't satisfied'.

Practical needs

'everyday important functions ... the tool that lets us tell the hair stylist to take just a little off the sides, direct the doctor to where it hurts ... ' etc.

In an interesting book, Robin Dunbar (see Further reading section) proposes that the first function of human communication is social gossip. The human equivalent of chimpanzees and gorillas socialising by grooming each others' fur. His researches indicated that 65 per cent or more of speaking time is taken up with social topics of one sort or another.

In fact, please think about your own communications every day. How many of them are important in the sense that they have a concrete product or outcome? Many do of course, and some of those outcomes are very important to achieve. Even successfully communicating 'two sugars please', is pretty important.

However, most of our communications with each other do not have a concrete product or outcome. Most of them are apparently purposeless, the 'hot air' of companionship:

- 'Brightened up again hasn't it?'

- 'Did you see it last night?'

- 'No, I didn't vote for him, didn't like his Tango.'

- 'I'm just off to the loo.'

- 'Have you heard what Irene did?'

- 'We went to the Safari Park at the weekend.'

- 'How's it going?'

Why do we say these things to each other? Because the first human need is just to be social, for the sake of being social. When we do this, communication is meeting those deep human needs listed above.

Intensive Interaction helps the person to develop all these communication abilities. First, the basic human need of communicating and being social for the sake of it, in order to fulfil deep human needs. Then for some, they will develop and progress to more concrete communications, including the development of speech and language. The amount of progress that each person can make, will vary greatly from person to person.

Let us conclude this introductory chapter by reminding ourselves again, about a theme that will run throughout this book. Communication fulfils all sorts of functions, some of which we have highlighted here. But the first is that it is enjoyable, interesting, wonderful, and that is the main reason for being a communicator.

Further reading 📖

Adler, R.B. and Rodman, G. (2006) *Understanding Human Communication*. 9th edn. New York: Oxford University Press.

Argyle, M. (1969) *Social Interaction*. London: Methuen.

Dunbar, R. (1996) *Grooming, Gossip and the Evolution of Language*. London: Faber and Faber.

Field, T. (2001) *Touch*. Cambridge, MA: MIT.

Hewett, D. (2011) 'Blind frogs, the nature of human communication and Intensive Interaction', in D. Hewett, (ed.), *Intensive Interaction: Theoretical Perspectives*. London: Sage.

Lakin, J.L. (2006) 'Automatic Cognitive Processes and Nonverbal Communication', in V. Manusov, and M.L. Patterson. (eds), *The Sage Handbook of Nonverbal Communication*. Thousand Oaks, CA: Sage.

Montague, A. (1986) *Touching: The Human Significance of the Skin*. New York: Columbia.

Senft, G. (2009) 'Phatic communion', in G. Senft, J.-O. Östman and J. Verschueren (eds), *Culture and Language Use*. Amsterdam: John Benjamins.

2

Background to Intensive Interaction

Graham Firth

This chapter looks at:

- **The history of Intensive Interaction**

  - **The 1980s – the start of Intensive Interaction**
  - **The 1990s – things move on**
  - **2000–10 – a new millennium**
  - **Into the future – 2010 onwards …**

- **What is Intensive Interaction?**
- **Who is Intensive Interaction for?**
- **What does Intensive Interaction teach? The 'fundamentals of** **communication'**
- **The nature of communication work in our services.**

The history of Intensive Interaction

The 1980s – the start of Intensive Interaction

In the 1980s the approach that was to become called 'Intensive Interaction' was developed by the teaching staff at Harperbury Hospital School as a teaching approach for people with what was then termed a 'severe mental handicap'.

The early development work on Intensive Interaction came about as a result of the teaching staffs' general rejection of the application of behaviour modification techniques with students with severe or profound learning difficulties. An action-research method was employed by the staff to help them look at ways in which they might improve their own teaching methods.

Before Intensive Interaction: prior to 1970 children with severe and profound learning disabilities were officially deemed to be ineducable. Then in 1970 came The Education (Handicapped Children) Act which gave all children a legal entitlement to an education.

At this time the main approach to teaching students with severe or profound and multiple learning difficulties was based on behavioural psychology, with widespread use of behaviour modification techniques. Then academic interest in 'infant–caregiver' interactions began to increase, eventually building an educational interest in these natural forms of communication and relationship building.

The staff team, most notably Dave Hewett (the then headteacher) and Melanie Nind (a dynamic young teacher who joined the team in 1985), started to think about how they might help their students learn or further develop their 'fundamental communication' abilities (Nind and Hewett, 1994, see Further reading section). In the early stages of the action research process the idea of creating an Appropriate Communication Environment (ACE) emerged. This ACE idea recognised the crucial need to be playful, light-hearted and naturally engaging in communication teaching with their learners. The Harperbury staff also started to use video (initially using the first commercially available camcorder, a Panasonic M1) to film their work. The film of the early ACE interactions was then used by the staff to look back and to analyse what was really going on in the interactions, and who was actually doing what and when (a revolutionary change at the time!).

At the same time Dr Geraint Ephraim, a clinical psychologist, was having similar ideas to the Harperbury team, and he characterised his approach as 'Augmented Mothering'. As Dr Ephraim's work looked similar to what they were doing themselves, some of the Harperbury staff met with Dr Ephraim and he encouraged them to continue their work and to read more about 'parent–infant' or 'infant–caregiver' interactions.

By 1986 the Harperbury team felt that their approach, now called 'Intensive Interaction', was well enough developed and sufficiently defined that it could be effectively communicated to other interested people. In 1987 Nind and Hewett gave a presentation on their work, 'Interactive approaches to the education of children with severe learning difficulties', at a conference held in Birmingham. This first general exposure of Intensive Interaction was soon followed by an article 'Interaction as curriculum' in the *British Journal of Special Education* (June 1988) which resulted in a great deal of interest in the novel approach called 'Intensive Interaction'. It was at this time that the generally 'bottom-up', practitioner-led dissemination of Intensive Interaction began, with Dave Hewett and Melanie Nind being invited to speak at a number of conferences and to give talks and training sessions to staff teams across the UK.

The 1990s – things move on

The 1990s saw the gradual dissemination of Intensive Interaction continue in services and schools across the UK. This process was helped by the increasing acceptance of 'person-centred' views of care, which identified people's needs on an individual basis. This made Intensive Interaction more relevant and acceptable to some services who had previously not considered using the approach.

In 1994, after Nind and Hewett had completed their research studies, *Access to Communication*, the first book on Intensive Interaction was published. After the publication of this book, Intensive Interaction became increasingly recognised and practiced in special schools across the UK. It also started to become widespread in some adult services. Also at this time international interest in the approach was just starting, initially with Dave Hewett visiting the Netherlands.

The 1990s saw the first Intensive Interaction research papers beginning to be published in the more academic type of learning disability and special education journals. These published research studies provided an increasing amount of scientific evidence supporting the claims made about the beneficial outcomes of using Intensive Interaction. This Intensive Interaction research covered work done with both children and adults.

In 1996 Phoebe Caldwell published *Getting in Touch* (Pavilion Publishers) which set out a description of her work using an 'interactive approach'. In this book she identified some of the parallels between her own work and Intensive Interaction.

In 1998 the second Intensive Interaction book was published, *Interaction in Action: Reflections on the Use of Intensive Interaction* (edited by Hewett and Nind), which included chapters by parents, carers and professionals on their day to day work using Intensive Interaction. This book clarified the purpose and practical application of the approach, and it gave the first multidisciplinary view of Intensive Interaction.

2000–10 – a new millennium

After 2000, with Dave Hewett continuing his unstinting dissemination and support work all over the British Isles, Intensive Interaction started to become much more widespread in schools and services across the UK (although there still remained some services where the approach was unknown). Also, interest in Intensive Interaction continued to develop in a number of countries worldwide.

In the early part of the new millennium, practitioners from various disciplines (including teachers, psychologists, and speech and language therapists) increasingly wrote up and published research studies and important position papers that significantly moved Intensive Interaction forward. At this time there were also a number of new books published, and the first video Intensive Interaction training resource *Learning the Language* (2002) was then released.

As the approach became more and more recognised and practised, in 2002 Dave Hewett and Cath Irvine (a specialist speech and language therapist from Somerset) organised the first UK Intensive Interaction Conference. This seminal and inspiring conference, attended by well over 200 delegates, was held over two memorable days at Birmingham University.

Leeds Mental Health NHS
Teaching NHS Trust

Intensive Interaction Newsletter

September 2003   Issue 1 (a real collectors item!)

News in Brief:

- Helen Elford has recently been appointed as Research Assistant for the project— Having met her I think we are very lucky to have someone of her undoubted talent to come and work with us.

- The Blenheim Centre, part of Leeds City Council's Inclusive Learning Service is now extending its use of *Intensive Interaction* for its students with profound and multiple learning disabilities.

- Dave Hewett was in Leeds recently providing a training day for the staff of the Trust's Children's Service

Dave Hewett

The *Intensive Interaction* Research Project nears a start (about time - ed!)

After meeting with almost all the home managers the *Intensive Interaction* research project has now identified the four NHS staffed houses in which *Intensive Interaction* is to be used as a means to promote sociability and fundamental communication skills for all it's tenants.

In these houses it is envisaged that all the staff will receive training and guided support in the use of *Intensive Interaction*, and will be given the opportunity to provide evidence to the project team of the successes, challenges and practical difficulties of using the approach in the social care setting.

The positive feedback about the potential for using *Intensive Interaction* was quite overwhelming, but unfortunately it was only possible to choose four homes due to the number of care staff in-

volved, and the practicalities of training and collecting evidence through interviews and questionnaires from the nearly 60 staff who work there.

This does not mean that training and support in the use of *Intensive Interaction* will not soon be made available to all other NHS staff who feel they could benefit from it. As soon as the initial work has been done with the research project staff, they further training opportunities will be made available more generally across the trust.

Harvey and Debbie exchange eye contact and facial expressions at the *Inclusive Learning Ser-*

Dave Hewett on the project

Dave Hewett, one of the originators of *Intensive Interaction*, said of the current project being run by Leeds Mental Health Trust:

' In the last fifteen years, awareness about the use and application of *Intensive Interaction* has been steadily growing amongst practitioners from all disciplines in the field of severe learning disability. Here is yet another milestone. I expect that the findings of the *Intensive Interaction* project will have wide implications, providing knowledge that will

be of benefit nationally.

How encouraging and uplifitng also to see the project producing its own newsletter. Please all take up Graham's call to put more people on the mailing list for the newsletter. The future challenge for those of us dedicated to the use of the approach is to continue the dissemination of this vital knowledge and here is an example of the sort of initiative that is needed.

All best wishes to Graham and the project team.'

Figure 2.1   Intensive Interaction Newsletter, issue 1

The Intensive Interaction Conference has now became an annual event in the UK, with these conferences giving an encouraging and supportive platform for a wide range of Intensive Interaction practitioners, advocates, professionals, parents and researchers to relate their own experiences and insights into the approach to many hundreds of delegates.

By 2003 the dissemination of the approach was starting to become more organised and far reaching. In this year, what has become the UK *Intensive Interaction Newsletter* was created by the then Leeds Mental Health NHS Trust, with its first tentative issue illustrated in Figure 2.1 (also see Chapter 10 for further details). As can be seen from this front cover, the first issue was mainly about local Intensive Interaction news related to the Leeds area, but since then it has taken on a more national, and even an international, character.

Also in 2003 things started to move into the digital age, and Intensive Interaction went online. The official Intensive Interaction website, www.intensiveinteraction. co.uk, was launched by Dave Hewett (again see Chapter 10 for further details).

In 2006 the *Intensive Interaction* DVD was produced by Dave Hewett. This DVD included footage of Intensive Interaction sessions conducted by practitioners in a number of contexts, including being used with children in special schools, and with adults in residential and day services.

It was also in 2006 that Dave Hewett, Cath Irvine and Graham Firth first worked together, setting out on a path that would eventually lead to the establishment of the Intensive Interaction Institute. With the help of many others, they endeavoured to define the purpose of such an Intensive Interaction Institute, this being to continue to define, develop and disseminate the theory and practice of Intensive Interaction.

In 2008 a more substantial international Intensive Interaction aspect started as the inaugural Australasian Intensive Interaction Conference was held in Brisbane. This conference was organised and hosted by Intensive Interaction Australia, this being especially dependant on the notable work of Dr Mark Barber and teacher Janee Williamson.

A year later Intensive Interaction Australia brought out an educationally focused DVD – *Exploring the Envelope of Intensive Interaction* – produced by and featuring Mark Barber and Karryn Bowen. This DVD contained some interesting and intriguing Intensive Interaction footage from Australian special schools.

In the UK Cath Irvine, alongside her work training Intensive Interaction practitioners and coordinators, started to organise a visible Intensive Interaction 'Community of Practitioners' within the spirit of the Intensive Interaction Institute. She started the process by suggesting and then nurturing the emergent Intensive Interaction Regional Support Groups across the UK (see Chapter 11 for more information).

An important Intensive Interaction milestone occurred in 2009 when the UK government policy document *Valuing People Now (VPN): A New Three-year Strategy for People with Learning Disabilities*, was published. This document explicitly stated that people with complex needs should have 'very individualised support packages, including systems for facilitating meaningful two-way communication' (on page 37 of *VPN*, DoH, 2009). This document then gave the whole next page over to an exposition of Intensive Interaction, and such explicit advocacy officially positioned Intensive Interaction as a mainstream approach that should be made available to everyone with a complex or profound learning disability who might benefit.

Into the future – 2010 onwards...

Intensive Interaction has already provided many people with an accessible approach that has transformed the way they work with and support people who had previously been socially isolated. Intensive Interaction has provided a clear working rationale for a wide range of people, including parents, teachers, psychologists, speech and language therapists, occupational therapists, music therapists, and many others.

However the future course of the approach will now undoubtedly be influenced by a range of issues – scientific, cultural, political and economic (possibly including some unknown issues yet to arise). But the most overriding factor in the further development and dissemination of Intensive Interaction will be the resourcefulness, energy and drive of the individual practitioners who use the approach.

It will be these individual practitioners, and the people who support and encourage them, who will further develop Intensive Interaction, thus building on the initial and seminal work that has already been done. Thus the history of Intensive Interaction will continue to move on, both individually and collectively, and everyone who can should look to play a role in that process.

What is Intensive Interaction?

At its simplest level Intensive Interaction is a process that aims to enable communication and sociable interactivity. Intensive Interaction is about being affirmative and sociable with people, even when this process is made difficult by the level or form of a person's communication or social impairment.

 Intensive Interaction usually occurs between a more skilled communication partner (which is probably you reading this book) and an emergent communicator who is still learning about communication and about the different ways to engage in social interactions.

Such an 'emergent' communicator will most usually be someone with a severe or profound learning difficulty and/or autism – however, Intensive Interaction is now being used with other groups of people who, for a number of different reasons might also be struggling with communication and being sociable.

Essentially Intensive Interaction is a process that involves two people trying to get along together, with them both trying to find common ways of communicating, even if these ways do not involve any words or symbols.

In Intensive Interaction, the more skilled communication partner is responsive to a person with a social or communicative impairment and they attempt to engage them in a number of ways that may help a sociable interaction to develop and evolve. This means that Intensive Interaction is a certain type of conversation between two people. Intensive Interaction is a conversation whose content is almost entirely decided upon by the emergent communication partner. Intensive Interaction is also a conversation in which the more skilled communication partner tries to be responsive to any communicative or potentially communicative behaviours of the emergent communication partner.

Thus with Intensive Interaction, both participants become significant contributors to an interaction, and they can also build a more equal and genuinely inclusive relationship. There is also a developmental or educational aspect to the use of Intensive Interaction. According to Dave Hewett and Melanie Nind (2001; see Resources at the end of this chapter), Intensive Interaction is 'an approach to teaching and spending time with people with learning disabilities, which is aimed specifically at the development of the most fundamental social and communication abilities'.

In Intensive Interaction the strategies used by the more skilled communication partner are based on those responsive communication strategies or techniques used by most adults when engaging sociably with young infants. All of us (or almost all of us) possess the required capabilities to carry through these communication strategies or techniques at some level. We usually use these techniques very naturally when we get along with most pre-verbal people that we meet; these tend to be the babies and young infants who we meet in our day-to-day life.

However, as you will see later, what you as the more skilled communication partner (or Intensive Interaction practitioner) will specifically do to enable Intensive Interaction to progress will very much depend on the individual characteristics and behaviours of the person you are trying to be responsive to and socially engage with.

 According to Melanie Nind (1996 see Some Important Papers section), Intensive Interaction has five central features, these being:

1. Looking to create mutual pleasure and interactive games within the interactivity – the communication partners being together with the purpose of enjoying each other.
2. The communication partner (that's you again) adjusting his/her interpersonal behaviours (for example, your gaze, voice, body posture, facial expression) in order to become more engaging and meaningful to the person.
3. Allowing interactions to flow naturally in time – with pauses, repetitions and blended rhythms.
4. Imputing 'intentionality' – crediting people with severe or profound and multiple learning difficulties with thoughts, feelings and intentions, and thus responding to their behaviours as if they have intentional communicative significance (even if they don't actually seem to have).
5. The use of 'contingent responding' – following a person's behaviour or communication lead and sharing control of the activity.

Who is Intensive Interaction for?

Intensive Interaction was initially developed at Harperbury Hospital School to address the learning needs of people with severe or profound levels of learning difficulties (a number of whom also had an additional diagnosis of autism). However,

Intensive Interaction is now seen as useful in developing the sociability and early communication skills of people from a number of different groups.

The people who are now seen as potentially benefiting from Intensive Interaction are those people who suffer from a severe social or communicative impairment. Intensive Interaction is also seen to benefit people who are socially very remote or passive (that is, who do not tend to initiate social interactions with other people) and people who engage in a variety of stereotyped or repetitive self-stimulatory activities, especially if these activities create some kind of barrier that prevents them from engaging socially with other people. Intensive Interaction is also used with people who experience severe multi-sensory impairments, who seem entirely unmotivated or uninterested in engaging in social activity.

In addition to these groupings, Intensive Interaction can be used with people who have already developed some symbolic speech and understanding, but who it is thought might still benefit from further developing their understanding of the more intangible aspects of human social interactivity.

It should also be realised that the benefits of Intensive Interaction go in both directions – the more skilled communication partner, be they family members, carers or support staff, also benefiting from the improved communication and social interactivity with the person they care for or work with. Even transport or escort staff – even the people at the corner shop – could, and perhaps should, be encouraged to get involved.

 A severe social or communicative impairment may be the result of a number of factors, such as:

- a severe or profound and multiple learning difficulties
- complex and multiple impairments
- autistic spectrum disorder (ASD)
- degenerative neurological conditions, for example, late stage dementia
- a serious acquired brain injury
- a socially impoverished or neglectful infancy, for example, when a child has suffered from severe social deprivation during their early life.

There are now, increasingly, reports and published articles on people from all the above defined groups indicating successful social engagement using Intensive Interaction with adults and children.

What does Intensive Interaction teach? The 'fundamentals of communication'

Generally, Intensive Interaction can be seen as an approach for providing people with positive experiences of being socially included and emotionally connected with others. As a result of these positive experiences, Intensive Interaction provides people with repeated opportunities from which to learn about 'doing' human communication and, subsequently, to acquire and develop the fundamental skills needed when being sociable with other people.

When Intensive Interaction was initially being developed, the participants involved were students who were still learning at the earliest developmental stages of communication. Thus Intensive Interaction was intended to facilitate the students in their learning of the most basic, non-symbolic communication skills and concepts that are generally learned before the development of representational speech, that is, before we learn to use abstract words and phrases.

These basic, non-symbolic communication skills and concepts have been called the *fundamentals of communication* (Nind and Hewett, 2001; see Resources). The fundamentals of communication collectively go together to make the most critical and foundational learning that all of us undertake, learning that is so vital and underpinning that if you do not make significant progress with this learning, then it is difficult to move on to learning other important things.

The fundamentals of communication are typically characterised as:

- learning about the significance of proximity and sharing personal space

- learning to give, extend and share attention with another person – then developing such shared attention into and across sociable or joint 'activities'

- learning how to have fun with other people – learning how to play

- learning how to take turns in exchanges of behaviour

- learning to use and understand eye contact and facial expressions

- learning to use and understand physical contact within social interactions

- learning about non-verbal communication such as gesture and body language

- learning to use and understand vocalisations, developing more varied and extensive vocalisations that gradually become more precise and meaningful

- learning to regulate and control emotional responses and arousal levels (Nind and Hewett, 1994; 2005).

These fundamentals of communication should therefore be seen as the first communication learning that any person can, and should therefore be expected to undertake.

In a wider sense, the learning outcomes associated with a structured and sustained use of Intensive Interaction (those fundamentals of communication again) might be seen to satisfy certain curriculum requirements for schools in 'developing communication skills for pupils who have difficulties with conventional speaking and listening' (p. 5, QCA, 2009).

According to UK government guidance, for pupils with severe or profound and multiple learning difficulties the school curriculum should aim to:

- enable pupils to interact and communicate with a wide range of people

- enable pupils to express preferences, communicate needs, make choices, make decisions and choose options that other people act on and respect

- increase pupils' awareness and their understanding of the 'world'.
  Planning, Teaching and Assessing the Curriculum for Pupils with Learning Difficulties – General Guidance, p. 5, QCA, 2009.

Intensive Interaction can help students achieve all these things!

The nature of communication work in our services

The learning of human communication is, in some respects, a highly complex process; although in some other respects it could be seen as relatively straightforward. Mostly, we all learn to be socially interactive by just doing it. In our everyday lives, starting from the point of birth onwards, we repeatedly practise and incrementally develop the skills we need to communicate and engage with the people who nurture and care for us – and we do this very naturally and without any fuss.

We also generally learn how to do 'human communication' without any requirement for SMART targets! (SMART standing for: **S**pecific; **M**easurable; **A**chievable; **R**ealistic, and **T**imed.) Instead, this process usually happens at just the right speed, and mostly it happens in just the right way – and the people who initially want us to learn about 'human communication' (usually our parents and close family members) let us naturally get on with it.

Not only do our parents and close family members let us get on with it, they also rather craftily use their natural parenting skills to help us do it – they are interested in us and they show us that they are. They look at what we are doing, and they encourage us to do more – they join in with us, and mostly they positively respond to us – with smiles and eye contact and happy noises, and physical contact and playfulness.

These caregivers are generally helpful when we struggle, they often wait patiently for us to take our turn, and they smile and laugh with us when we succeed – sometimes they even tease us and tickle us and pull funny faces at us. But what they do not tend to do is look to mark us or to judge us against a set of SMART targets.

However this is not always the way it works when we come to a lot of educational settings – sometimes special schools and further education services feel the need to push communication teaching ahead too fast. In doing so, they can put too much emphasis on acquiring abstract and symbolic communication skills, before the necessary fundamentals of communication that underpin the communication process are fully rehearsed and thus properly learned.

Such a pressure to develop a person's symbolic language can often be applied for a variety of good reasons – wishing to promote a learner's independence (for example, being able to ask for something like the 'toilet' or 'a drink'), or trying to help someone indicate a preference ('If you want a drink, do you want "tea" or "coffee"?').

However, the reason might also be as much to do with getting someone with severe or profound learning disabilities to perform some observable 'communication' task that can then be ticked off on a 'communication' checklist.

Possibly such symbolic communication teaching is given priority over other types of communication learning because it is relatively straightforward to measure, and thus relatively easy to satisfy a school's requirements for observable 'evidence' of successful teaching.

That is not to say that symbolic communication skills are not very important to learn when the learner is developmentally ready to do so. However, we should always have as a main aim for our pupils or students that they continue to practise and thus continue to develop their fundamentals of communication. Even if they are less easily quantified and difficult to set SMART targets for!

Continuing to rehearse and further develop a learner's fundamentals of communication through the use of Intensive Interaction should never be seen as secondary to the teaching of signs, symbols or objects of reference.

Further reading 📖

Department of Health (DoH) (2009) *Valuing People Now: A New Three-year Strategy for People with Learning Disabilities* available at http://www.dh.gov.uk/en/Publicationsandstatistics/Publications/PublicationsPolicyAndGuidance/DH_093377.pdf

QCA (2009) *Planning, Teaching and Assessing the Curriculum for Pupils with Learning Difficulties. General Guidance* available at http://orderline.qcda.gov.uk/gempdf/144590022X/P_scales_Guidelines.pdf accessed 6 April 2011.

Resources

Nind, M. and Hewett, D. (1994; 2005) *Access to Communication: Developing the Basics of Communication for People with Severe Learning Difficulties*. London: David Fulton. This book, the first and still the single most significant publication on Intensive Interaction, sets out a clear conceptual framework for understanding and using the approach.

In 2001 *A Practical Guide to Intensive Interaction* by Nind and Hewett was published by the British Institute of Learning Disabilities (BILD). This book was deliberately written as an accessible guide to the approach, and set out the latest thinking and practices associated with Intensive Interaction.

In 2002 the first Intensive Interaction training video, *Learning the Language* by Phoebe Caldwell, was published. This video showed Phoebe using Intensive Interaction with a young man with severe autistic spectrum disorder. The video also includes footage of support workers discussing and using Intensive Interaction with some of the people they care for.

In 2003 *Implementing Intensive Interaction in Schools: Guidance for Practitioners, Managers, and Coordinators* by Mary Kellett and Melanie Nind (David Fulton Publishers) was published. This book gave structured advice on how Intensive Interaction could be used in schools within the constraining guidelines of the English National Curriculum.

Some important papers

Firth, G., Elford, H., Leeming, C. and Crabbe, M. (2008) 'Intensive Interaction as a novel approach in social care: care staff's views on the practice change process', *Journal of Applied Research in Intellectual Disabilities*, 21: 58–69.

Kellett, M. (2000) 'Sam's story: evaluating Intensive Interaction in terms of its effect on the social and communicative ability of a young child with severe learning difficulties', *Support for Learning*, 15(4): 165–71.

Leaning, B. and Watson T. (2006) 'From the inside looking out – an Intensive Interaction group for people with profound and multiple learning disabilities', *British Journal of Learning Disabilities*, 34: 103–9.

Lovell, D., Jones, R. and Ephraim, G. (1998) 'The effect of Intensive Interaction on the sociability of a man with severe intellectual disabilities', *International Journal of Practical Approaches to Disability*, 22 (2/3): 3–9.

Nind, M. (1996) 'Efficacy of Intensive Interaction: developing sociability and communication in people with severe and complex learning difficulties using an approach based on caregiver-infant interaction', *European Journal of Special Needs Education*, 11(1): 48–66.

Samuel, J., Nind, M., Volans, A. and Scriven, I. (2008) 'An evaluation of Intensive Interaction in community living settings for adults with profound intellectual disabilities', in the *Journal of Intellectual Disabilities*, 12(2): 111–26.

Watson, J. and Fisher, A. (1997) 'Evaluating the effectiveness of Intensive Interaction teaching with pupils with profound and complex learning difficulties', *British Journal of Special Education*, 24(2): 80–7.

Watson, J. and Knight, C. (1991) 'An evaluation of Intensive Interaction teaching with pupils with severe learning difficulties', *Child Language, Teaching and Therapy*, 7(3): 10–25.

Zeedyk, S., Caldwell, P. and Davies, C. (2009) 'How rapidly does Intensive Interaction promote social engagement for adults with profound learning disabilities and communicative impairments?', *European Journal of Special Needs Education*, 24(2): 119–37.

How do human beings start learning to communicate?

Dave Hewett

> **This chapter looks at:**
>
> - **How babies communicate**
> - **How communication and interaction develop.**

In Chapter 1 we briefly looked at the wonderful scope of human communication abilities. Human communication takes place at high speed in various 'channels' – sound, vision, touch and smell. Our communication abilities are complex, elaborate, intricate, detailed, multilayered, multifaceted and enjoyable. There is general agreement that the learning of being a communicator is the most complicated learning that human beings do. I have already emphasised in Chapter 1, how incredibly complicated is, for instance, face-to-face communication.

Yet, as we must all be aware from our own experiences, learning to be a communicator is the first learning; it starts on day 1 for all of us (actually, recent studies point to the beginnings of communication learning taking place within the womb as well). I often make the joke that since this learning is so complicated, surely it would be better to leave it until you are about 18 and have more experience of life?

Think about the average 1-year-old child if everything is going well. Think about how quickly this person has developed as a communicator. How do babies accomplish this remarkable feat of learning the most complicated stuff – a vast body of knowledge – and so quickly?

Luckily, we live in an exciting age when science has started to understand how babies do this. There are two main reasons:

1. During the first year, well throughout babyhood, babies' brains are 'hot-wired' for conducting this learning. They are going through what is termed a neurological

'hot period', where their brains are sort of 'on fire' for doing this learning and their brains develop quickly as they receive the right experiences.

2. We know however, that if babies are not placed in the correct environment, none of this learning will take place. The *correct environment* is the 'teaching' that adults do with babies. Of course, we do not mean teaching in its traditional sense. The teaching and the learning mostly takes place during the natural, beautiful, pleasurable interactions with babies. I jokingly call it the 'gooey' times that most of us cannot resist having when a baby is near.

The rest of this chapter will focus on the 'gooey' times, those natural interactions. There is a good reason for this of course. Intensive Interaction was developed by looking at the research on how those interactions function. If we could achieve a practical understanding of how they work, there might be all sorts of helpful principles we could use in our work with people who are older, but nonetheless at a stage of development where their priority is to learn the same things.

During the late 1960s, child development research started to shift its focus. The work on early childhood learning in particular started to look at the way in which learning and development did not take place in isolation *within* the infant. Rather, early learning and development is primarily a joint enterprise. It takes place within shared social situations between the baby and the available adults – principally the parents.

It was increasingly recognised that social and communication development was mostly taking place in paired, mostly face-to-face situations where the main thought was to enjoy being with the baby, and vice versa. As the 1970s arrived, so did helpful equipment for studying these developments. The 1970s brought the era of usable video cameras, video cassettes and, therefore, the possibility of using slow-motion and freeze-framing. This was exactly the right technology for the researchers who wanted to study the complexities of parent–infant interaction. Most of the research tended to come from, and still comes from, the USA, but there have been notable studies in the UK too.

Babies learn the complexities of communication during enjoyable, relaxed interactions with adults

The literature in this field is vast and complex. However, reading and analysing it brought about a summary of general principles that became influential in the development of Intensive Interaction. As you read the list below, try to think about your own experiences, either as a parent, or incidental experiences you have had with babies.

General features of interactions with babies:

- The main motivation for both people is mutual enjoyment.

- The interactions vary in length between a few seconds and many minutes as the baby develops.

- Even within the first few weeks, babies can learn to take part for several minutes at a time.

- The main early accomplishments are learning to give and share attention, eye contact, finding faces interesting, learning turn-taking, indeed the structure of dialogue and conversation, vocalising, initiating, being powerful and leading, and gradually speaking, using words.

- The nature of the interactions develops gradually but quite quickly under their own momentum through the first year and by the second year are likely to be 'branching out' and including all sorts of toys and activities.

 The increasing emphasis on the perception of the infant as an active participant in a process of learning and *rehearsing* how to be a communicator was reflected in a well-known early work by Colwyn Trevarthen (1974) from Edinburgh University: 'Conversations with a two-month old', *New Scientist*, 896: 230–5.

Of course, from an Intensive Interaction viewpoint, the most interesting issues concern how the interactions *work*. Literally, what are the processes that get the activities going and support them. In particular, what does the adult do and how does she or he do it?

Features of the adult style during interactions:

- The adult does not have an objective or a predetermined end point they are working towards.

- The adult does not lead the interaction and 'drive' it along.

- The adult tends to hold her or his behaviour back, waits and watches for the baby to do something.

- Therefore there is a sense of the baby being in the lead of the activity.

- When the baby does something, the adult responds or joins in.

The adult uses lots of imitation and 'joining-in' with what the baby does

- There are therefore many pauses, with the adult watching and waiting.

- The adult responses can be delighted face, delighted body language, delighted voice, running commentary, and so on.

- The most frequently seen adult response is imitation/copying, joining in and doing what the baby just did.

- If there is a really good moment created, the adult might attempt to extend it and keep it going, perhaps by repetition.

- There can be, of course, frequent and/or sustained physical contact, and that channel of communication is very important for a baby.

There are three advantages for the baby of the adult style:

1. The tempo of the activity is OK, the baby can deal with it – in fact since the baby more or less leads, it is the baby's tempo.

2. The content of the activity is understandable for the baby – the baby generates most of the content.

3. The adult's behaviour is not too complicated – because the adult does so much imitating and joining in, the adult is behaving more like the baby than a complicated adult.

If you have not encountered this analysis of parent–infant interaction before, did that ring bells of familiarity for you? Most people have some sort of reaction along the lines of, 'Oh yes, I knew that really, I just didn't quite know it consciously'. Most of us will behave in this kind of a way when with a baby without consciously thinking: 'I have to hold back now, wait for him … and then … yes, he's done something so now I will imitate it.'

We do it probably mostly non-consciously, like much of our face-to-face communication with everybody, as outlined in Chapter 1. However, in Intensive Interaction, we may do much the same sort of thing, but actually, more consciously and deliberately. We might use these principals more tactically.

So, the system of baby communication development rests on babies having these interactions frequently and repetitively. Repetition is a word you will need to get used to from now on in this book. It is reckoned that in any single interaction between an infant and parent, most of the activity is repetition of things they have previously done in interactions.

However, day by day, the activities grow and develop – expand. They gradually expand in duration, they gradually expand in content and they gradually expand in sophistication and complexity. For instance, in the second half of the second year, words and speech are likely to make up quite a bit of the content of an interaction.

Of course, by the middle of the second year, babies' learning is branching out from these attainments in all sorts of directions, and they are starting to do things with objects, be interested in the physical world generally and learn a great deal by observation. However, the abilities and skills they are now using have come about from cognitive and neurological development during the interactions. Furthermore, these interactions and the learning that comes about during them will continue throughout the rest of their early learning.

Further reading

The most famous book where much of the early research is contained in one volume is:

Schaffer, R.H. (ed.) (1977) *Studies in Mother-Infant Interaction*. London: Academic Press. There are other famous names within the book: Jerome Bruner, Barbera Beebe, Daniel Stern, Kenneth Kaye, Colwyn Trevarthen and Hanus Papousek.

Part 2

Practicalities of doing Intensive Interaction

In the next six chapters, we describe what we can call the absolute 'nuts and bolts' of how to do Intensive Interaction. Literally what do you do, what are the techniques?

There are two main possibilities for your starting point:

1. You are starting with a person who is at a very early stage of being a communicator and does not make social contact easily, or is very isolated.

2. Your person already has some ability to relate and be social, so you have some already developed activities which you can enjoy with her or him.

Also, you may or may not have some knowledge and experience with an Intensive Interaction practitioner.

We are going to write our description of how to do Intensive Interaction starting from absolute point 1 (above), that is, from the point of view that you are an inexperienced Intensive Interaction practitioner starting off with a person who has little communication ability.

We then proceed slowly through the process of establishing the activities, then developing a sense of progress and progression with the person and the activities, together with associated issues such as teamwork and recording.

If your starting point is more like point 2 above, then you will be picking up on the progression of the activities with the person somewhere further along the 'continuum' of Intensive Interaction development that we outline below – perhaps at a point around Chapter 6. You will probably not be so concerned with issues such as 'making access' or 'establishing activities'.

However, we suggest you read from the beginning anyway. We have attempted to pack these chapters full of useful advice. Maybe there is something you have missed out on in your work so far.

4

Preparing for Intensive Interaction

Dave Hewett

This chapter looks at:

- the principles of Intensive Interaction

  - What help do we take from looking at the 'natural model' of infancy?

- what Intensive Interaction sessions are like

  - Simple, enjoyable activities
  - Intensive Interaction activities or sessions can take many forms
  - The activities develop and change
  - What equipment or resources do we need?
  - Intensive Interaction practitioners do need a flexible range of behaviour
  - Principles not 'rules'
  - Planning or preparation for activities?

- preparation

  - Who are you going to do Intensive Interaction with?
  - Mental preparation
  - Write a programme or scheme of work?
  - Finding one-to-one time

- observation

  - Do a baseline?
  - Video

- Preparing the team?

  - The whole team goes for it together?
  - Or the team goes for it perhaps one by one?

The principles of Intensive Interaction

What help do we take from looking at the 'natural model' of infancy?

We can observe and identify principles that are present in the way that parent–infant interactions work that can be useful to us. We can therefore write below a straightforward list of principles that are at the heart of doing Intensive Interaction activities. If you simply do these things, Intensive Interaction will happen. We will add more detail to this list as we proceed through this chapter, but these are the core principles:

- **Quality one-to-one time**: Like parent–infant interaction, Intensive Interaction usually takes place in situations where the two people have time to focus on each other. As we will illustrate later, this does not necessarily mean going somewhere quiet and private.

- **'Tune-in'**: you, the teacher, the more experienced person, will sensitively 'tune-in' to all the feedback signals from the other person whether from voice, facial expression, body language, movement or gesture. Everything you do will be based on reading the feedback from the other person.

- **Tempo/speed**: Go slowly, and basically hold back your behaviour to allow the other person to be in the lead and to take the lead.

- **Responsiveness**: You build the content and the flow of the activity by responding to things the other person does.

Intensive Interaction is focused, quality one-to-one time

- **Imitation/copying/joining-in:** is the most frequently seen way of responding. This is easy to do and it helps your person to understand that what you did was in response to what she or he did.

- **Use simple behaviour:** Try to keep your behaviour very simple and uncomplicated – using imitation/copying/joining-in usually makes sure of this.

- **Pauses:** Be prepared at all times to pause, wait, allow the other person time to think and process and have the activity happening at a comfortable speed. Try to resist the desire to 'drive' the activity forward.

- **Mutual enjoyment:** The main motivation for the activities, the main reward for taking part in the activities, for both people, is enjoyment. Be prepared to find the activities enjoyable. Expect to enjoy yourself.

It is easy to see that you can develop some activities by borrowing these main principles. Many practitioners in our work 'discover' how to do Intensive Interaction because of their personality and their natural behaviour style. They may not even know they are doing Intensive Interaction – this way of being just feels natural and right to them.

So, what are Intensive Interaction sessions like?

Simple, enjoyable activities

Let us remind ourselves of what we are setting out to achieve. It is basically the same learning and outcomes as in parent–infant interaction.

The idea is simply, to create turn-taking sequences with the person of extended, enjoyable shared attention. The main motivator for being in the activities is the sheer, natural enjoyment.

We might look upon these activities as nothing more than creating a 'conversation' with the person. A conversation that might not involve many words, but involves exchanges of interesting behaviour they can understand and enjoy.

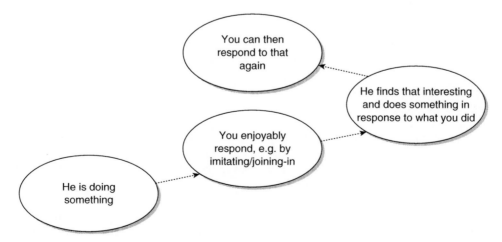

Figure 4.1   Simple diagram to illustrate the creation of turn-taking

These activities, perhaps simple and brief at first, transform and develop into longer, more sophisticated, more complex periods of shared, mutual attention and exchanges of behaviour.

Within these experiences, the complicated learning of communication routines and skills and being social takes place. The learning is very complicated, the activities feel simple. We do this in the first place by being responsive to what the other person is already doing, already knows, not by being directive and telling them what to do. Therefore, each activity is created more or less, by the responses of the two people, moment by moment.

You might expect that the activities will be 'free-flowing' with a great deal of variety in what takes place. They can be quite varied, but it is worth remembering and recognising how repetitive they can be. Owing to the nature of the learning for a person who is at an early level of development, the activities can be highly repetitive. Your person's preferences and needs can cause you to do the same sort of interaction activity over and over again.

You can frequently hear it said that what we do with Intensive Interaction is to go and join the person, sensitively, in their world, on their terms, and start doing things with them based on what they already know, understand and feel comfortable with.

Intensive Interaction activities or sessions can take many forms

They can be lively, playful, noisy, happy, fun, enjoyable. They may also be quiet, thoughtful, peaceful, but meaningful and enjoyable.

Sometimes, the activities can be an intense exchange of vocalisations, just like any conversation between people who know each other.

The activities can be very playful and energetic, a physical romp even; or they can be quiet, still, serene.

The activities develop and change

Intensive Interaction 'sessions' can gradually change, from:

- specific times set aside for early try-outs, but members of staff hopefully also taking advantage of any incidental occurrences

- early successes growing into identifiable sequences of interaction that are often repeated over and over

- the person growing and developing within these interactions

- the progress of the work with the person gradually bringing about changes in the communication performance of the person

- the gradual changes in the content, the quality and the variety of the interaction sessions developing into an ordinary but full aspect of the social environment. Intensive Interaction will probably not only be something you set time aside for, it just happens as part of that person's social world.

But first, you will likely be devoting specific time to be available to your person in a one-to-one fashion for a few minutes – some say a 'session'.

What equipment or resources do we need?

The main teaching resource, the main equipment will be you – you the member of staff, the more experienced person, the communication partner, the teacher.

Your resource is your face, your voice, your body language, your sense of presence, your personality, your way of being.

 Technique point: the best piece of equipment

What is the best resource or piece of equipment in your home or workplace?

YOU

A person – face, voice, body language, personality, sense of presence.

What is the best piece of equipment in your home or workplace? It is not the touch-screen or the interactive whiteboard. It is you, a human being. You are the most intricate, flexible, ingenious, wonderful piece of equipment on the surface of the planet. Nothing else can do what a person can do.

You will be using yourself, flexibly and enjoyably to create frequent free-flowing activities with your person.

You are the main equipment. However, anything else – any object, toy, piece of furniture, household equipment – can also be equipment, and using it can form part of the content of the interaction.

Intensive Interaction practitioners do need a flexible range of behaviour

You do not need to be an extrovert to do Intensive Interaction. Actually, some people who are extrovert talk about how they can often get carried away and do far too much in their responses – go 'over the top'.

Some members of staff talk about learning how to be 'silly' or do 'silly' things, the need to lose or deal with your inhibitions in order to be an interaction partner. Sometimes people who are more reserved more easily develop a simple, 'deft touch' in their interaction style.

Perhaps being prepared to have a natural playfulness is a better way of putting it. The reality is that there is nothing particularly strange about Intensive Interaction behaviour; you simply find a way of behaving that makes sense to the person you are communicating with.

It is a good idea to remember always how varied human behaviour can actually be and to recognise the sorts of behaviours that can be interesting and meaningful for

The teaching and learning is relaxed and enjoyable

people who are at early levels of development. You adapt to that person and find a communication style that works and that is understandable to them.

Principles not 'rules'

In all of the description of how to do Intensive Interaction in this chapter, we will only rarely tell you exactly what to do. 'Exactly what you do' is something you and/ or your interaction partner in collaboration, decide on a moment-by-moment basis. The activities are as free-flowing as that.

All of your processes of thinking and decision-making are dependent upon your reading of the person and the situation, moment by moment. So, we cannot tell you exactly what to do, moment by moment. However, we can tell you all of the Intensive Interaction principles. These principles will guide you in how to be, how to behave and, to some extent, how to decide, in order to think your way through Intensive Interaction activities.

There is a danger that describing it like this makes it sound complicated. It is not. Describing Intensive Interaction in words always runs the risk of making it sound more complicated than it is.

Having outlined all of that, here is one rule that is worth describing right now. We will return to it on several occasions in the following text. It is simple.

When the other person, the learner, has had enough, the activity should stop.
If the person is not in the mood or the right frame of mind, probably do not start.

Planning or preparation for activities?

For some of the reasons outlined above, it is difficult to make a firm plan in advance for what will take place during an Intensive Interaction activity. Indeed, this is not a good idea. One of the main principles above is that the other person, the person who is learning, leads the activity with her or his behaviour.

You develop the content and the flow of the activity by responding to what she or he does. If you have planned and decided in advance exactly what will or should take place, you are less likely to have this main principle operating properly.

 Intensive Interaction is a process-central approach

For the learning to take place, you do not need to set session objectives and work towards them. Rather, the objective of the session is to activate the process where the learning takes place.

The process is the two people becoming engaged with each other, and sharing and exchanging a flow of behaviour.

But, as we said above, repetition is a key feature and it is likely that both interaction partners will find the repetition of successful activities to be enjoyable.

As you get used to this, and the whole process develops with a person, you start to realise why firm planning in advance is not necessary. The activities develop a spontaneous flow and momentum of their own. They activate increasingly easily and you start to understand the way that developments and progress come from this natural momentum.

However, you should go into each activity feeling prepared for the way the activity works. In the sections that follow, you should find plenty of advice on preparation.

Preparation

Who are you going to do Intensive Interaction with?

One of the main issues in preparation is thoughts around who you are going to do Intensive Interaction with. As you read this there are probably two main possibilities:

1. You are working with an individual who stands out in your mind in terms of concern for her or his welfare and this person is uppermost in your mind when thinking about doing Intensive Interaction.

2. You are working with a range of people whose abilities and understandings are such that they are all people for whom the approach would be suitable.

If 1 above is you, we would highly recommend going easy on yourself. If you are a new Intensive Interaction practitioner, you should pay particular attention to all the places here where there is advice on relaxing, being realistic, not berating yourself if things are not happening according to your hopes and expectations.

If 2 applies to you, there are some options you could think about. If you are new to doing Intensive Interaction, we would generally advise that you start working with the person who you judge might respond most readily.

This may be a person with whom you already have some established activities and enjoy being social. It is understandable that the person who is alone in the corner might be giving you the greatest concern and is your main motivation for reading this book. However, you might consider that you will help her or him all the more easily, if you first take care of yourself by consolidating your expertise with other people.

Mental preparation

The first thing you need to take care of is you. You cannot rush into doing Intensive Interaction. You cannot make it work better by trying harder or putting more effort in.

Take time; take as much gentle time as you can in commencing this work.

If you are reading this book, you are already doing some thoughtful preparation. You might also like to do some other reading or view some of the DVD materials. This will help.

Then there is some psychological and emotional preparation that can be carried out. That might sound strange, but it is not. If you are a member of staff, a practitioner, you are probably embarking on Intensive Interaction work because you care very much about your work and the welfare and well-being of the people you are working with.

If you are a parent, relative or friend of the person with whom you will be doing Intensive Interaction, then you care passionately about their well-being in every regard. You also have a huge understandable need for her or him to relate and communicate with you more fully. We suggest the logic of doing Intensive Interaction with a person is obvious.

Case Study

'I've found out how to have proper quality time with the guys. I never realised how much they don't get quality time with us. They get loads of attention from us lot – but it's all around tasks and doing things. Proper quality time with a person is just being together for the sake of it. Yeah, I think I've learnt about quality time for myself too.'

Member of care staff, residential establishment

The main mental preparation is to beware being impatient to achieve progress. Progress with Intensive Interaction comes about all the better if we relax and allow the gentle unfolding of the process to do its work.

Try not to feel urgent and 'urge' things to happen. This is a very common reaction from practitioners new to Intensive Interaction. Bringing urgency and stress into the situation is counterproductive. Being relaxed and flexible is productive.

For practitioners in this field of work, there is an issue we all deal with around achieving progress with the pupils or service users. Many practitioners seem to feel very stressed by the pressure they are under to achieve tangible results. That stress and the sometimes urgent practices that can arise from it will be the enemies of good Intensive Interaction work.

Do not feel guilty about slowing down during the day. Do not feel guilty about taking more time over things, taking more time to just 'be with' your pupils or service users. Do not feel guilty about doing things with them where there is no task to fulfil or finish. Be glad about these things.

As a team, you might like to read this section and discuss these issues as part of your preparation. Most practitioners we meet in most services recognise that they are doing or being asked to do too much in the available time.

Write a programme or scheme of work?

The degree to which practitioners write schemes of work varies from service to service. However, these days the writing of detailed individual programme plans (IPPs), individual curriculum plans (ICPs) or individual education plans (IEPs) is general. Just because Intensive Interaction does not employ session objectives, this does not completely remove the need for paperwork and planning.

In fact, we suggest it is really important that you establish the seriousness of what you are doing, or attempting to do, by writing it up in just the same way that you write documents for all other areas of work with your people.

 If you have not already done so, this really is the time to enlist the collaboration of your speech and language therapist. Of all the professionals who work in support of 'front-line' staff, they are most likely to have knowledge, expertise and experience with Intensive Interaction. Speech and language therapists have been prime movers in the establishment of the approach over the years.

We have suggestions about documentation in Chapter 7.

However, we also acknowledge that at this stage you might be a practitioner who just wants to read this book and have a go at doing Intensive Interaction. You might be working in the sort of team where at the moment you do not want to share the 'project' or cannot share it. You just want to try it out without fuss and bother.

If so, fine. Do not worry, do your thing and get yourself feeling comfortable with the earliest stages of being an Intensive Interaction practitioner.

Otherwise, we make this suggestion. Even if you are trying Intensive Interaction as something brand new, it can be a good idea to write a little document that outlines:

- what you are trying to do

- how you are doing it

- what the outcomes may look like.

It does not need to be a big document at this stage, just a couple of sides of A4 that you can immediately offer to the person who asks: 'What is this all about? What are you up to?' You can answer them verbally of course, but we always suggest that it is a signal of being an authoritative practitioner if you are able to give them the message: 'Here, read this. I've thought about it quite a bit.'

Finding one-to-one time

We keep saying it but an effective Intensive Interaction practitioner is a person who is relaxed, attentive, 'tuned-in' and unhurried.

So, if you are a practitioner in a workplace, the first thing you might need to do is to start thinking about how you will find or create quality one-to-one times. Remember, you are going to need lots of it.

 Quality one-to-one time

Finding or creating sufficient, quality one-to-one time can be difficult in busy work places. See Chapters 5 and 6 for discussions and advice on this issue. If you are a parent, Chapter 9 is concerned with some of the issues around doing Intensive Interaction at home.

So, start finding or creating these times. You and your team might already have well-established routines of making sure that everyone receives good quality focused attention.

If you are a parent or working with a person at home, there should be plenty of opportunity already for relaxed 'down time'. Yet, some residential establishments can have a rather stressed, task-orientated atmosphere these days.

It is sadly the case that in many special schools, especially, there has been a focus in recent years on group work and teams may have lost both the ethic and the practice of one-to-one time with each pupil. If that is the case, then you might need to have a good think about establishing these times within the routine. You are already facing some changes to the way that you do things. We make some suggestions in Chapters 6 and 7. This might also involve team or work-place discussion as part of the period of preparation.

In those chapters and elsewhere here, we additionally make the point that doing one-to-one time does not necessarily mean, for instance, leaving the classroom to go to a quiet room. Going somewhere quiet can be necessary in the early stages with people who are difficult to reach, anxious and easily distracted. It can also be an interesting, routine aspect of the work, at any time with any person, to also have activities somewhere quiet and private.

However, if you are going to establish Intensive Interaction as occurring regularly and frequently enough to achieve progress, then the majority of the activities need to take place within the normal, regular situation. Also, this person's communication routines cannot be something that only happens on special occasions in a special place. That does not feel like the right atmosphere. Intensive Interaction is not something special that needs to be done in a special place at a special time. Intensive Interaction is ordinary communication for that person.

Case Study: *More one-to-one time*

Ivan was 13, with multiple disabilities. Once the team found out how to do Intensive Interaction with him, they no longer toileted him. Instead, they went into the bathroom with him and had a really good communication session, fun, relaxed, often noisy. While they were doing that, he went to the toilet.

(SLD classroom team)

With people who have high support needs, we can remember that we already have masses of one-to-one time scheduled into the day. We have to help them with all sorts of routine care and assistance, for some of them with every aspect of daily life.

We can view helping a person to eat, wash, go to the toilet, also as valuable one-to-one times where Intensive Interaction can take place – even during and throughout the giving of this routine care.

So you may already have, or have achieved by hook or by crook, the availability of some one-to-one times. But do not yet do Intensive Interaction, use the time instead for a period of observation.

Observation

Intensive Interaction is a subjective way of working. What we mean is that when you are interacting, you 'tune-in' to the person, you use all the facilities of your personality, your awareness, your ability to find shared communication moments from often small occurrences.

You operate tactically, using your powers of observation and decision-making sensitively to find the right moment. You find out how to 'time' your behaviour and responses.

You also work intuitively, using your inner, often non-conscious communication resources in much of the way that we described in Chapter 1 with human face-to-face communication generally. The quantity of the blend of conscious and intuitive, non-conscious working varies from person to person. However, with practice and experience most people find themselves working increasingly intuitively.

So before starting, spend some quiet times doing a subjective observation of the person you will be interacting with. This literally means sitting and enjoying that person. It does not necessarily mean distancing yourself or being aloof, but instead taking time to just let yourself enjoy the way this person is, the way she or he behaves, letting your unconsciousness learn this person's behaviour and possible communication signalling.

Most practitioners in our work are very good at putting to one side all artificial notions of human 'normalness' and accepting that human beings are also capable of engaging in a wide range of behaviours – for example, rocking, flapping, tapping, spinning, vocalising, skipping, moving continuously, sitting still and staring, seemingly endless repetitive behaviours of all sorts, and so on.

All of us in our work surely come to accept that doing all of this is quite normal for some people, and that people can be tremendously different from one another in their behaviour. That is part of the purpose of the observation, to learn the intricacies of this individual's individual behaviour.

Start thinking about which parts or aspects of the person's behaviour or way of being offer you opportunities for responding to her or him. Remember, you do not have to respond to everything the other person does.

Take the time to start the feeling of tuning-in to the person, especially the aspects of your responsiveness and communication performance that will feel intuitive or non-conscious.

 Conscious or non-conscious responses

> Intensive Interaction practitioners can be all sorts of personality types. We all vary in our mental processes as we carry out Intensive Interaction activities.
>
> Some people seem to be very natural, highly intuitive and empathic, hardly seeming to give Intensive Interaction any conscious thought, seeming to do it easily. Others are more conscious and tactical in the way they go about Intensive Interaction, thinking their way from moment to moment.

Just the same, during some of these observation times, you might like to hold a video camera. Watching the footage afterwards can give you all sorts of information and insights that you did not see in real time in real life.

During this observation period, you can also start to develop some plans. This will mostly take the form of thoughts like, 'oh that little movement with his arm he sometimes does, I'll try joining in with that', or 'she makes that little rhythmic vocalisation frequently; I'll gradually try responding to that, imitating it carefully'.

Again, let us make the observation period unrushed, enjoyable and thoughtful.

Do a baseline?

A baseline can be various things, but it is basically a series of recordings and observations that establish and define how the person is and what their abilities and communication performance are like at the start of your Intensive Interaction work.

You can do a baseline to various degrees of technical detail and precision. However, in most respects in most work places, the sort of baseline procedure we outline here will be sufficient. This will provide a general, fairly accurate summarisation of the person's ability and performance at the start.

Video

Now is the time to start shooting videos. Shoot some (three or four) general videos of the person while they are on their own. Five minutes' worth of footage is fine.

Also shoot three or four videos of the person with members of staff in general communication situations. These will be the usual interactions where there are opportunities for the member of staff and the person to connect and communicate.

There is no need to do any particularly technical analysis of the videos. Their first function will be for straightforward visual comparison with videos shot at a later time where the difference in the person's communication ability should be clearly apparent.

In Chapter 7 you can find detailed advice on record-keeping. This covers tips and techniques for shooting and editing video footage.

You can find a section on use of video and consent issues in Chapter 9.

There is also extremely helpful advice on using video in Mary Kellett and Melanie Nind (2003) *Implementing Intensive Interaction in Schools* (London: David Fulton). If you do not work in a school, do not be put off by the title, much of it will still be useful to you.

Preparing the team?

The extent to which you do preparation for the rest of your team at this stage will vary from practitioner to practitioner and situation to situation. We work with many, for instance, speech and language therapists who find themselves in the position of 'hero-innovator'. They can find it necessary to get the work started without help from members of the team, due to some of the reasons outlined below.

There are also various care practitioners who work solo in various situations such as within the home of the person. Other practitioners might need to go it alone, even though they are in a team. In this book we stress how natural and ordinary Intensive Interaction is. It is also one of the few approaches in use in our field that is actually based on scientific analysis about how human beings naturally learn things.

Many of you who are reading this may be parents. You may be in a situation where you spend a great deal of time on your own with your son or daughter and that will be the situation for you in setting up Intensive Interaction activities.

(Continued)

(Continued)

Tandy Harrison offers advice from her own experiences as a parent and practitioner in Chapter 9.

You may also be parents viewing this section from the point of view of seeing yourselves very much in a team situation – mum, dad, brothers and sisters all wishing to have a go at establishing further happy interactions with your son or daughter. We give advice on team issues throughout the book. This is of course, primarily aimed at our practitioner colleagues. We nonetheless hope that there is much that is useful and usable in your 'team'.

Yet to many services, teams and individual practitioners, Intensive Interaction can still feel like something new, different and radical. It may therefore not be possible to enlist the cooperation of colleagues in doing something new and different.

The situation may be one where you feel you want to do your try-outs without flagging it up to colleagues. You may be feeling that your Intensive Interaction work is something you wish to get the hang of in a relatively discreet way, without a great deal of attention from perhaps, sceptical colleagues. You want to try it out, do your experimentations, learn and become confident, without that constant attention and even criticism from other colleagues.

You may feel that your ability to disseminate your Intensive Interaction work to others will be all the better once you have gained confidence and a sense of expertise. You may also feel that you can gain their attention and commitment all the better by showing some outcomes in terms of progress that your person has already achieved.

The whole team goes for it together?

If on the other hand your team-working situation is such that you want to take colleagues with you and get them 'on board' right from the start, there are various suggestions listed below for hopefully interesting and inspiring them:

- Be open about what you are intending to do – ask people whether they have knowledge or experience of Intensive Interaction.

- Start incidental discussions on, for instance, 'How much communication work do we actually do?' Bear in mind the issues we have covered in Chapter 1.

- Share round or copy for colleagues any handouts on Intensive Interaction from courses you have attended.

- Show some or all of the Intensive Interaction DVD in a staff or team meeting. Leave the disc in the staffroom.

- Leave this book in the staffroom.

- Enlist the cooperation of various colleagues in establishing the baseline 'assessment'.

Or the team goes for it perhaps one by one?

Even if you work in an effective team situation where you have colleagues always immediately at hand, say a special school classroom or a small residential house, you need to make a decision.

> In the very beginning, do you want to do all the initial try-outs yourself without contribution from these colleagues then sort of generalise to others?

Or

> Do you want to organise it so that the whole of your little team is having try-outs in some sort of agreed rotation?

Either approach has merits and disadvantages. There is no way to advise you on the right decision. Basically we would say that if you already have a good teamwork ethos and you are comfortable with each other, go the second route. Get everybody going together with a happy sense of collaboration.

However, there can be organisational or practice issues that cause you to decide on the former. One of the frequently asked questions is something like: 'Is it better to have one member of staff or several doing the Intensive Interaction work with a person?' The answer is a general, 'It's better for it to be a small group of staff, not too many at first'. The reasons for this are:

- If you are working with a very 'difficult to reach' person, the 'access' stage can take time. A small team can support each other, review together and pool ideas. One personality may make a breakthrough owing to something in her or his personality.

- Even as the interaction activities get going, it seems clearly advantageous for the person to have a variety of potential experiences available from a variety of personalities.

- When the person learns something new with one member of staff, she or he has an immediate opportunity to generalise the usefulness of the piece of learning to other people.

- A team approach seems to guard against the risk of too much emotional bonding with one person.

- It also addresses any atmosphere of rivalry and exclusivity – 'Well of course, I can do that with him, but none of you can'.

So, after a good, comfortable period of relaxed observation and preparation, let us move on to the next chapter and thoughts about getting going with Intensive Interaction activities.

Further reading

Hewett, D. (2011) 'What is Intensive Interaction? Curriculum, process and approach', in D. Hewett (ed.), *Intensive Interaction: Theoretical Perspectives*. London: Sage.

Resources

The Intensive Interaction DVD is available from the Intensive Interaction website: http://www.intensiveinteraction.co.uk/.

5

Getting going

Dave Hewett

This chapter looks at:

- **Starting: making access**

    - **The person is truly 'difficult to reach'**
    - **The person presents as seeming to be very difficult to reach, but actually is not**
    - **The person is quite social and available, but undeveloped as a communicator**
    - **Realistic expectations**

- **Having your first attempts**

    - **Responsiveness ideas and the 'available' look**
    - **Where to be? Placing yourself**
    - **Try out some ways of responding**
    - **Examples of making access**
    - **Do you prompt or initiate in order to get things going?**
    - **First success**
    - **No observable success in the first and subsequent early try-outs**

- **Early success and progress**

    - **Consolidating your first successes and gradually moving on**
    - **Keep going with what you have established**
    - **Getting the 'feel thing'**
    - **How do Intensive Interaction activities end?**
    - **The person gets very excited, the activity can get out of control**
    - **Flow and mutuality.**

Starting: making access

'Making access' is a phrase that describes the process of you finding the first moments of interaction that work to cause the other person to become interested in what you did in response to them. It also means that you can probably succeed in creating this shared interest consistently – you have made some access to her or him, and he or she has a feeling of access to you.

We describe below three of the most usual possibilities for starting points with a person.

The person is truly 'difficult to reach'

The first reality is that getting the first feeling of success can take time. This is particularly the case if you are working with an adult who has probably had a life of social isolation or very limited real daily contact since she or he was tiny.

You need to remember that this person has many years' experience of living in a complicated world and adopting a set of behaviours and a lifestyle that works – or is at least reasonably effective for getting them through each day. Whatever you do in order to win her or his attention has to compete with that 'inner life'. This can also still be the case even if the person is a young child with only a few years' experience of social isolation.

The person presents as seeming to be very difficult to reach, but actually is not

On the other hand, sometimes a person who seems quite distant, detached and presenting as very 'difficult to reach' can sometimes 'light up' and take interest in what you are offering, then start making clear daily progress almost immediately.

This can be a somewhat surprising turn of events, even causing you to feel a little unsettled. Very quickly, you have to re-evaluate your concept of this person. There can be immediate sensations of 'Oh why didn't we do this before?' This can be emotionally disturbing for you, and you may even feel guilty.

Sometimes, the reality truly is that it is not the person who is difficult to reach; it is us that are difficult to reach for them. Often in our standard working practices we can continuously behave in ways which make us complicated and unreachable creatures.

Try not to feel guilty and blame yourself if you find yourself in these circumstances. Read Chapter 2 and take heart that this can happen to all of us in all of our working circumstances. Be glad that you have arrived at this realisation and then really go for it with opening up this person and her or his world.

The person is quite social and available, but undeveloped as a communicator

The third reality is that people can have a history of being in services where all of the experiences available do not address or make access to their ability to learn to be better communicators. So the person might be someone who is quite lively and aware and interested in the people around her or him.

However, she or he might have relatively limited communication skills and routines. They can frequently therefore develop some limited, often repetitive, but from their point of view nonetheless meaningful, ways of interaction with staff.

You probably feel keenly that this person could and should have more well-developed, and more detailed knowledge of skills as a communicator.

Realistic expectations

So, as previously described, we are taking the description of doing Intensive Interaction from the point of view that you are starting with someone who is still at a very early stage of development, does not speak, indeed does not successfully make very much contact with other members of staff or anyone else.

This is the part of the process where, if you want to use the word, 'patience' can be a virtue. In fact, patience is probably not the right word. Everything here is about realistic expectations. If you have realistic expectations, you do not need to be patient. You will be realistic.

There is a spectrum of possibilities for what can take place in this initial stage. Remember:

- with some people making first access can take minutes or even be immediate

- with some it can take days

- with some it can take weeks or months.

Your first attempts

Responsiveness ideas and the 'available' look

You are going to have your first attempt at an Intensive Interaction session with the person. The basic idea is very simple. You place yourself in a position where it is possible for you to do something, an enjoyable response to the other person's behaviour, so that the other person notices it. Your job is to tune-in so that you notice the other person's moment of attention to you.

From your observations, you probably have some prepared ideas about things you can try. Fine, use those ideas, try them out, but do not close your mind to possibilities that present to you on the spur of the moment. Do not forget to take time, go slow, go easy on yourself. 'Switch-on' your best 'available look'.

 Technique point: the *available* look

The 'available' look is quite difficult to describe in words, but it is about adopting non-threatening, relaxed, open, available body language, facial expression and sense of presence. You look, to the person, totally available and prepared to be 'enjoyably used'. One practitioner said it looks like you are ready to thoughtfully 'consult'. In fact, a person who has a good available look also looks like they are open to enjoying themselves.

Do not forget to be prepared to enjoy yourself – have that as a part of your available look.

Try to start tuning-in to the person before you approach. We use the word 'approach' advisedly. You may decide not to be particularly near to the person at first.

Where to be? Placing yourself

There are various possibilities to think about with regard to placing yourself in relation to the other person. Most videos about Intensive Interaction will usually show the two people being physically close. Intensive Interaction also can involve a great deal of physical contact.

It is true that on the whole these communication exchanges tend to work better when the two people are close together, but it is not an absolute rule.

Intensive Interaction can also take place with the two people some distance apart, or even on the move – walking, running, crawling even.

 Technique point: get lower

If you are comfortable with being in close proximity with the person, try this. It really helps her or him to give you attention, particularly to give attention to your face and eyes, if you get physically lower. This does not need to be way down lower, several feet, though this can work. No, if you simply get your eyes and face at a lower level, so that the other person has the sensation of looking *down* at you.

Try this, it really helps. The human psychology is surely obvious.

Even if your person is socially 'difficult to reach' you may have a well-developed relationship where being physically close to the person is not a problem. Therefore your starting point may well be approaching with sensitivity and starting to try things out from close by.

On the other hand, you might make the judgement that in these early stages, it is better not to be too close to the person. Some reasons may be:

- The person is 'difficult to reach', anxious and nervous about other people's proximity. This can particularly be the case with some people who have ASD.

- The person may be very difficult and unpredictable and you have some anxieties about what she or he might do on the spur of the moment.

- You are attempting to interact with a very energetic person who is constantly on the move.

Try out some ways of responding

So, if you feel that you are in a good position, try out some ways of responding to the other person's behaviour. You do not have to respond to everything the other person does; you can select items or parts of their behaviour.

Getting lower can really help communication

Remember what you are trying to achieve and observe happening for the other person: a moment of attention from the other person, the realisation that their awareness has 'locked on' to you however briefly, because of the interesting or intriguing thing that you did. If you are lucky at this early stage, you might quickly create that sequence of what we can call 'social cause and effect' explorations.

What are you looking for as you respond? Well, something that the other person does that shows interest in what you just did. Perhaps a recognition even that what you did was because of what *he or she* had just done.

 Technique point: it is a good idea to video early try-outs

If you can do the organising and you feel confident, it is a good idea to shoot videos of early try-outs of Intensive Interaction with a person. It gives you the potential to see two things particularly:

1. Anything you missed in real time. Lots of things show up better on the video, plus you can use slow-motion.
2. You can review yourself and your technique. Remember, be positive about what you do right.

A teaching assistant taking part in the early work on developing Intensive Interaction described this as, 'I'm just trying to see that what I did has "lit him up" a tiny little bit at least – then I know I'm sort of *in*'.

Remember, do not do too much at first, do not do it all in one go. It is particularly useful and important to use pauses here. Try a response and leave a good long pause.

Try not to get anxious or urgent. You may feel that the other person should respond within 5 seconds or so. But that is probably *your* need based on the speed of interacting you are accustomed to with fully-fledged communicators.

Case Study: *Nearly missed it*

Nika finally saw it in the video of her last try-out with Jermaine. It was when she said, 'OK Jules I'm moving on now, see you later'. Jermaine made a noticeable little flick of his hand and a nod of his head. It was difficult to see in amongst his movements and mannerisms, but it looked real in slow-motion. So, she tried it again next session.

Do not forget that what the other person does in response to you may be something tiny. It may also be something not immediately recognisable as a communication. Part of the job is at this stage to stay tuned-in for these things.

It may particularly be the case that people with ASD can do very tiny, subtle or unconventional things as a response. They may also do these things very fast. People who have ASD may frequently have very lively minds and well-developed speed of thought and movement, even though they are socially distant. They may do something very tiny, very quickly as a response. They may do it several times, but then get fed up with the fact that us silly fools are not picking it up.

While you are the crucial piece of 'equipment' in these activities, it is fine to use any object as part of the interaction content – any toy, thing, object, any part of the physical environment. It is also not against the rules to use speech, even if the other person does not understand. Sensitive, crafted little statements from you can be part of the way you respond.

Any type of object can also be part of the content of an Intensive Interaction activity

Technique point: using objects?

We have emphasised quite a few times that the main resource and the best piece of equipment for Intensive Interaction is you, the interaction partner. It is what you do with the marvellous and creative complexity of your responses that allows the activity to happen.

However, that does not mean that you do not use objects. Any object can be a good focus for Intensive Interaction activities. Read the examples in these pages. You can see that many of the people we work with have favoured objects that they use in their behaviour style – Lego, a book, sand play, a radiator. It is a natural option for us to join in with the behaviour involving the object.

There is also no reason why you should not have a range of objects available in the immediate environment. These would be thoughtfully chosen things you know from experience may be of interest to the person. If they pick up on one of them it provides you with an opportunity.

At times you might also introduce objects, though do it with the kind of care we outline in Figure 5.1: The two scenarios (p. 56). In fact, probably the best way to introduce an object is to have it easily available for the person to decide to become involved with it.

Technique point: how much speech should I use?

There is not one answer to the question, 'How much speech should I use as part of my way of responding and interacting?' You can observe a wide range of differences in the styles of people doing Intensive Interaction. Sometimes you can see a range of differences among different members of staff interacting with the same person. Yet the interactions seem to be equally successful for all of them. The same question has been posed by the researchers studying parent–infant interaction, partly coming up with the same answer – that the quantity of speech used can vary a lot among different adults when interacting with babies. With fast-developing babies, one of the major issues is likely always to be that they will be quickly moving on to understanding, then using speech, so it is important that an amount of speech input is present.

This issue applies to Intensive Interaction with older people also. Many of them will have the potential to develop to some speech and language ability. You cannot always predict who that will be. So, yes it is important that speech is present, but it is also important that the speech input is balanced and considered. Once again it is about constantly tuning-in to the feedback from the other person in order to guide you in your thinking. However, here also is a list of points to consider:

- Using little bursts of running commentary is always an available, effective way of responding – 'Did you like that?' 'Yeah that's right.' 'Oops, dropped it.' 'Oh yeah, this is good.'
- Keep it simple.

(Continued)

> *(Continued)*
>
> - Especially in the early stages, the tone of your voice is probably at least as important as the content of your statements.
> - Some people are very inexperienced, very withdrawn, very anxious at the start. When interacting with them it is often important to be constantly thinking, 'Keep it simple, don't do too much'. Quite often it can be easy to put more of our own behaviour into the situation than the other person can comfortably handle. These thoughts might lead you into limiting your speech or deciding not to speak, at least for the moment.
> - Equally, sometimes something in the way the person seems to attend to your voice leads your intuition into putting much more speech input into the situation, even though this person seems to be at early stages.

If nothing seems to be working at first, do not keep going relentlessly. Take a rest, move away, collect your thoughts. It is best to stop while you are still in good shape and not tired. Remember, we do not expect success straight away. With some people this 'first access' bit can take months.

But come back to another try-out relatively soon. If you are already in the sort of team situation where you are all doing try-outs, talk together, review, watch each other.

Stay optimistic but gently determined. You will get there eventually. Remember it is not the other person who cannot do it, it is us who simply have not found the way yet.

Examples of making access

This section offers a wide variety of examples of 'making access' situations. We hope it fully illustrates just how different it can be for different people and how much we as interaction partners need to be flexible and free-thinking.

Case Study

Tanya would sit on the window sill tapping the radiator. Ulla started by sitting on the floor with her back on the radiator. When Tanya tapped, Ulla tapped. Tanya tapped – one second – Ulla tapped. This went on for a few minutes, then Ulla realised it had become conversation. Tanya wasn't just tapping, she was now tapping in response. This was confirmed when Tanya tapped twice and laughed when Ulla followed suit. The speed of development of the game was so quick that day and the next, Ulla couldn't believe they hadn't done something this simple before.

Case Study

Trevor would stand in the playground with his fingers in his ears staring at his reflection in a window. He was almost vibrating with the intensity of what he was doing. I would approach slowly and he didn't mind if I stood next to him. I would put my fingers in my ears and stare in the window. Eventually, after quite a few days, I realised Trevor was looking at my face, maybe making eye contact in the reflection. One day the next week he turned his head and looked at me, but quickly away again.

Case Study

Anne lay on a mat or beanbag. She couldn't seem to move at all. She didn't seem to be able to see, either, and they weren't sure how well she could hear. Neela insisted that members of staff should spend long attentive minutes lying against Anne, so that she could, hopefully, at least feel their presence.

When Neela took her turn, she liked to get everything quiet if she could – ask the others to turn off the music. This was because Neela liked to touch heads and listen carefully to Anne's breathing pattern. Neela started following and emphasising Anne's breathing, constantly working at her timing to try and make it clear to Anne that she was doing this. Very gradually, Neela started to believe that Anne was deliberately breathing with emphasis, or changing the timing, in order to experiment with Neela's response.

Case Study

It felt easy. Jeannette grabbed hold of my hair and said 'Hah!' I said 'Hah!' She said, 'Hah'. We did this 20 times or so and eventually she let go of my hair and we just said 'Hah!' – 'Hah!' Three weeks later we've moved on to 'Hah hah', 'Huh', 'Argh' and 'Eh'. She presses foreheads now for eye contact.

Case Study

Sean was always constantly on the move – running, jumping, skipping, up and over furniture, window sills. It seemed logical to give him plenty of time in the school hall; in fact, this time was something of a way of surviving the day with him. When Beatrice joined the team, she was surprisingly enthusiastic to take on the job of accompanying him. However, she had ideas from previous experience. Beatrice simply sat on the floor in the middle of the hall. Every time Sean's route took him past her, she would sit up, beam at him and say 'Hiya'. Gradually, after a few days, she reckoned he was coming past her more frequently and there was a better quality of direct look as he came past.

Case Study

'He likes these dinosaur figures, well loves them really. He's always got one. He likes to tap them against his chin, looks really thoughtful. So each day I would get one and sit with him, tapping my chin. He seemed to think that was great and look at me much more, much better …'

Case Study

Ben is 5 years old, has a diagnosis of ASD and seems very distant. He liked to stay in his corner, jumping up and down, flapping his arms and hands laughing and smiling at the ceiling. The team always had a terrible struggle with him to get him to come out of his corner and sit down at a table to do 'activities'.

Then Marion read a book and tried something different. On the Monday morning, she went to Ben's corner and simply joined in with his jumping, flapping and laughing. Ben responded immediately, giving Marion full attention and sharing the 'game'. He took her hands and they jumped and laughed. It was so easy. After a few days, Marion and the others could do this activity with Ben for many minutes. He would hold hands, make eye contact, shout a 'more', pull them onto the floor and clamber onto them. Six months later he takes part in most things with confidence, and uses about 10 words from time to time.

Case Study

'I don't know what I did really … Just sort of sat near him in a nice, kind way . . . Sat for a long time, saying something quiet now and again … Used to do this a lot … then I think he started leaning against me and playing with my fingers … then he would turn and look at my face … it's just grown from there.'

Case Study

Kris would sit for a long period of time cross-legged with several pieces of Lego on the floor between his legs. He would constantly fiddle and rattle them together on the floor while staring at them. Eva simply got some Lego, and sat near him and copied what he was doing. After a few days and 10 or so try-outs, she could see that he was starting to look at her fingers and her Lego. Sometime the next week he looked up into her face and leaned towards her slightly.

Case Study

When the team received Louisa, she was a tiny 5-year-old, curled constantly into a tight human ball. She seemed to be completely deaf and completely blind and had been neglected and left to herself almost since she was born. She was resistant, tactile defensive and completely uncooperative.

They had to use touch but she hated touch. Eventually, Valanie found an 'in'. The starting point was the merest clicking of fingernails together. Valanie did a Scenario 1, took the first turn, clicked Louisa, then waited, waited. Louisa did not seem to be distressed by this tiny touch. Valanie tried again 1 minute later. At last, one time, after many attempts, Valanie had to wait only 10 seconds and Louisa extended a finger, found Valanie's hand and fingernail and clicked in return.

Case Study

'Claude would sit all day in his wheelchair grinding his teeth. We all found it kind of tough to be around. I'm dentist phobic – so teeth grinding – agggh! He couldn't do much else I suppose. He couldn't move much, didn't see too well, but his hearing, as it turned out, is absolutely fine. Some of us went on an Intensive Interaction course, came back with some ideas. We talked about it and started spending time just sitting with Claude. We worked out that we didn't have to grind our teeth, we could just make a clicking noise inside our mouths when he did his grind. We were astonished at how quickly this became knowing turn-taking. Then he started sitting up straighter, turning toward us, grabbing us ... He must have been so bored for years.'

Case Study

'I did the most obvious thing. I just stood near him and joined in with his flapping and rocking and his sideways movements around the room. He didn't seem to mind, but I wasn't sure he was taking any notice. I must say I found it fun anyway though – I think I started to realise why this way of behaving felt good to him. Anyway, after about 10 days of four or five times a day, I started to identify that his head turned more towards me and that when he moved slightly sideways he would kind of wait, looking at my feet and legs for me to follow.'

Case Study

Radi sat and rocked, moving his head in little semicircles, his eyes seeming to focus vaguely in the distance. Rosemary sat in front of Radi and just slightly to the side, slightly lower. She joined-in with his rocking and rotating his head. She and Annette did this four or five times a day each. After some days, Annette became convinced that Radi was orientating his head rotations more towards her, and his eyes seemed to be focusing on her, interested.

Case Study

Jamal was 23 and presenting as a person at a very, very, early level of development. He was somewhat mobile, moved around slowly and he was a bundle of 'sensoriness' and tactility. In his way he was very social, constantly seeking out staff to cuddle-up to, lean against, or tap fingers and hands or sort of squirm his forehead into their shoulders.

There was debate, some felt that his initiations and his physicality was not appropriate. Others pointed to the actual reality of his psychological and emotional development. Eventually they rationalised that way more or less. The more 'accepting' members of staff were given licence to go with their viewpoint. It was easy really to create many different turn-taking games with him quite quickly, he was already so available and initiating so much.

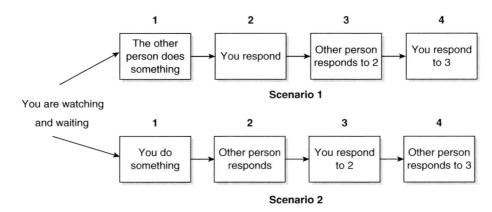

Figure 5.1   The two scenarios for getting turn-taking going

The only difference is who takes the first turn. When you take the first turn (Scenario 2), as long as you are not insistent, you are not being directive. You are not violating the principle of responsiveness. If you do it right, with good tuning-in and sensitivity, you are simply gently and carefully prompting the other person (1) into doing something (2) to which you can then respond (3) and so on.

Do you prompt or initiate in order to get things going?

In Figure 5.1, we outline two scenarios for turn-taking sequences. As you can see, the scenarios are simple enough; the only difference between them is who takes the first turn.

There generally seems to be a pattern in the development of Intensive Interaction activities with a person. In the earliest stages, following the principle of letting the person who is learning be in the lead, means that you will pretty much stick to doing Scenario 1. You hold back your behaviour, give the other person time and space to think and decide to do things.

Therefore, you do lots of pausing and waiting, tuning-in, looking for the moment, the opportunity. In these early stages, even as you get things up and running, with turn-taking sequences starting to happen easily, it is still likely that you will be relying on Scenario 1.

This is not an absolute rule by any means – sometimes we take the first turn by doing something without even being aware of it, and the other person responds. For instance, as the activities develop, it can happen that simply moving near the person causes her or him to 'light up' in anticipation. You then immediately have that behaviour from her or him to respond to.

When you use a Scenario 2 and do something first, take the first turn, it is important to remember you are not being directive. In a sense you are not even taking the lead. You are simply making a suggestion, a gentle prompt. You are offering an idea for the other person to take up. The best style is this. If your initiation does not work, do not get stuck on it, do not insist; move on.

It is generally the case that as the person moves on and develops and becomes more involved in regular Intensive Interaction activities, the use of more Scenario 2s evolves quite naturally. On the whole you do not even have to think about it consciously, they just arise as part of the natural, happy flow. Even when things are well developed with easy interactions happening and flowing regularly and with all sorts of outcomes becoming apparent, the majority of sequences will still be Scenario 1.

So, on the whole the advice would be, in these early stages, to try to resist the temptation to prompt and nudge and make things happen. Relax and take your time and give Scenario 1s plenty of time.

There is a technical reason for all this, concerned with the person's learning and their sense of personal power. There is a tendency in our work for services to have traditionally developed highly directive practices with people. This is partly because of the praiseworthy desire to direct them towards useful learning of concrete accomplishments. It is also, we believe, because services and practitioners have historically not given enough time and perhaps ingenuity to helping the person become motivated to initiate, do things, to have personal power.

Case Study

'Yeah, well in the early stages, it seemed like he just wasn't going to join in or do anything unless I took the initiative and led him into it. So I did frequently and it sort of worked. We started having some enjoyable play-type activities, romping and rolling, noisy. But even now a few months on it doesn't happen unless we start it, he still just sits until we get it going. So we're sort of trying to go back over the early ground now, start again and slow down a bit more.'

Intensive Interaction reverses that trend. Intensive Interaction, right from the start of activities with a person, crucially takes time to help that person find the spark, the motivation to take part and be stimulated. The major aspect of achieving that is for practitioners to use sensitive, observant Scenario 1s in the early stages.

This enables the first major learning outcome for the other person. 'I can do social initiations – I can be positively powerful.' If we are taking the lead and as usual prompting or directing the person into taking part, this once again prevents that learning.

If you are not getting early success, it is best to keep trying things briefly, but frequently and regularly.

So, there are two main possibilities for what can happen in the early stages:

1. Success – your first early try-out starts to work a little straight away.

2. In your first and then subsequent early try-outs you are not able to observe anything you can identify as success.

We will deal with each of these possibilities in turn.

First success

What will the first moments of success be like? There is a wide variety of possibilities. The stories in the previous sections should illustrate that variety.

First, basically, you find a moment or moments when there is an often small response or recognition from the other person. She or he has briefly, as we say, 'lit up'. What do you do next, literally in the next instant?

Well, if you are not too taken by surprise, of course responding to that moment of attention is the very best idea, do something to 'mark' the moment and convey that you have seen the possible connection. There are of course, many possibilities, for example:

- a widening of your facial expression, your eyes and mouth 'lighting up' even more

- a vocalisation – 'Ahhhh', 'Yeah', 'Hi'

- a movement of head, shoulders

- imitate/copy/join in with the lighting-up behaviour of the other person

- anything that your intuitions tell you feels right

- or simply repeat the response that caused the interest.

These are simply examples, suggestions. You use your judgement, intuition and natural behaviour in order to decide what to do next just as much as remembering any advice from reading this book. Remember, the main piece of equipment we are using is you and your existing knowledge about how to be a communicator, and gear all of your communications differently to each different person.

It could be the case that you start to get a sensation of lift-off, with some more tangible development in the progress of the interaction right there and then.

Your response to her or his moment of being 'lit up' causes her or him to respond in turn once more – you are already having a brief turn-taking sequence (Figure 5.2). Or it could be that this moment will be all the progress within that session and you are looking for further progress and development gradually in other sessions.

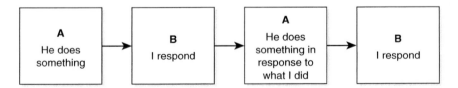

Figure 5.2   Simple early turn-taking sequence A-B-A-B

Do not forget also, allow yourself to be really pleased. This is what you are working towards.

No observable success in the first and subsequent early try-outs

As said previously, do not get despondent. Be realistic; it can be expecting too much that this person will start taking part in the activities easily and quickly. Keep up the momentum of frequent, regular daily try-outs. Be flexible, be imaginative and creative with what you try.

But also, do not hesitate to repeat the same response many times – it could be that your person needs plenty of repetitions of that response in order to 'read it' and become familiar with it. Once more, let us remember that any such repetitions should be carried out sensitively.

However, do not just 'drive' the same response *at* the person, do 'tuned-in' reading of her or him to make sure that, at the least, she or he is not in any way discomfited by what you do. This is the sort of situation where it helps to have more than one member of staff doing try-outs with the person. If the work is shared, you can watch each other; different personalities try different things. One person might achieve some success because of something in their personality, but with observation, the rest of you can 'borrow' that aspect of technique.

It is really helpful to do some written evaluations or weekly round-ups (see Chapter 7).

Also, it is incredibly useful to use video recordings reasonably regularly. Shoot videos of various try-outs and then try to find time to watch the videos carefully. Again, doing this as a group exercise is beneficial – a team-building exercise, a bonding of your team's thoughtfulness on communication issues.

There are a range of possibilities for what you might identify from some video evaluation:

- You might see responses from the person that you missed in real life.

- You might even see that the person is actually giving you quite good quality attention and you are not picking it up in real time.

- You might see some further opportunities within the nature or flow of the other person's behaviour when you are nearby that you did not see in your earlier observations.

- You might identify that you are going too fast, too slow, not being sensitive enough, or accidentally doing things with your behaviour that are unhelpful.

Important things to remember through a long period of trying out ways of responding:

Remember.

Small is BIG.

For the people we are working with, a new development that is something tiny, is something big for them.

- Stay positive by being realistic – with many people it just does take time to get the activities established and up and running.

- We have previously outlined some reasons for the above but we do not fully understand why this is so for each individual person.

- Do not be hard on yourself; you may be going through a period of learning how to do what you are attempting to do.

- Keep reviewing and evaluating as objectively as you can – is your person actually making some tiny responses or bits of progress that you are failing to recognise? Or, have you noticed some changes but not acknowledged that they are significant?

Early success and progress

Consolidating your first successes and gradually moving on

You have made some 'access' with the person. You have some shared activities. You are still in the early stages, but the possibilities for what is taking place in these early stages are actually quite wide and vary from person to person. Let us try and put that into a diagram briefly showing a continuum of possibilities (Figure 5.3).

Figure 5.3 describes three possible situations, and your work with your person could be anywhere along that continuum in the early stages. If your situation is more like C in the diagram, well congratulations, you are going great guns. You are working with a person who was actually raring to go and probably has been for some time.

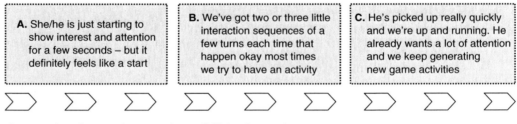

A. She/he is just starting to show interest and attention for a few seconds – but it definitely feels like a start

B. We've got two or three little interaction sequences of a few turns each time that happen okay most times we try to have an activity

C. He's picked up really quickly and we're up and running. He already wants a lot of attention and we keep generating new game activities

Figure 5.3   The continuum of possibilities for early progress

It can be the case that some people with ASD particularly, can look and present as if they are very detached and difficult to reach. Yet, when the right, understandable social opportunities are made available to them by an Intensive Interaction practitioner, they can spark up and take off quickly. If this is your situation, go with the flow. Some people make progress so quickly you might have the sensation that you are almost struggling to keep up.

Case Study: *The same activity over and over*

'Yeah, development was very slow at first. We just seemed to do the same little hand-patting activity over and over. She would do it with all of us. Not a lot at first but after a couple of months she wanted to do it a lot. The same thing over and over.

We got a bit bored with it really and it didn't seem like there was any change. We didn't feel that Carrie was making progress at all, she was just stuck with this activity.

Then gradually we could see that though the activity was the same all the time, Carrie was gradually changing. She was doing it much more relaxed, less frenzied. She was looking at us more, smiling more and sort of a better smile – during the hand-pat activity.'

Case Study: 'Let's go'

'We simply were not anticipating the sudden developments. It was almost like Ferdi exploded into life in a burst of energy and communicative happiness. I've supported quite a few teams doing Intensive Interaction but I haven't seen somebody react like that before. He went from being a very isolated person, flicking and skipping, very quickly to this demanding interactor. He was actually kind of creative in the number of different interaction activities he generated. It was as if he got the hang of it and said to us, "lovely, let's go". He could also keep in the activity for about 20 minutes, right from the start.'

Indeed, their sense of intense joy because of these new connections may be a little overwhelming for you. It is a good idea to be prepared for these outcomes. There can be some distinctly emotional outcomes. This may be the case for the person you are interacting with, but it can also affect you. Emotional issues are addressed in various sections of the book.

Within our description of the processes of getting Intensive Interaction established with a person, you have quickly moved on to the next section in our book. Do not stop reading here though.

So, keep up input, try to give that person as much time and as many sessions as you can. Remember our observation in Chapter 2, that few people actually receive the optimum quantity of input in terms of numbers of Intensive Interaction activities.

Crucially, also keep up observation and record-keeping.

The rest of this section assumes that you are more likely to be somewhere between A and B in Figure 5.3.

Keep going with what you have established

Things are happening. You have some small developments. A little activity or two are established that you can repeat successfully and your person takes part relatively easily. You may have a small range of members of staff able to take part in the activities with the person.

You may still be in the situation where you have to be quite sensitive – you need to spend time finding the moment with the person and getting the activity going every time by doing the same responses to her or his behaviour. This gradually attracts her or his attention and activates the activity.

Or, simply approaching her or him causes recognition and anticipation of this recently found interesting activity and she or he deliberately starts up.

Again, a caution about working too hard to get things going every time. But have this activity as frequently as you can, remembering:

1. The activity stops the moment you sense that the person has had enough.

2. If your reading of her or him tells you that she or he is not in the mood, or this is not the time for whatever reason, then do not attempt to start.

 Technique point: repetition

Repetition is good.
People at early levels of development like repetition.
Repetition provides familiarity, predictability, a sense of safety and security, a sense of control and expertise.
Repetition provides plenty of practice of very complicated learning.
Repetition provides structure.
Repetition is part of the main 'engine-room' of forward progress for the person within Intensive interaction activities.

Do not worry about doing the same activity over and over again. Considering the situation the person may have been in for some years, doing a single activity that feels safe and successful over and over again is not an unreasonable desire. It is logical that they may want this. They may be very enthusiastic to do an activity many times if it feels interesting, enjoyable, safe, secure, stimulating and it allows them to at last, cross the social bridge to other people.

Progress can nonetheless come within the same activity with developments in the person's abilities, even though the activity itself does not apparently change much. But progress, of course, also comes from the development and expansion of the activity into a wider variety of interactions and content. The priority for this period is to get the activities and the sense of gentle lift-off solidly established.

Do some session evaluations if you can, session evaluations are as much about helping you with confirmation of your growing technique as they are about recordings on the other person.

Shoot videos if you can – review and evaluate them, preferably with colleagues. Remember – positively. Evaluations are positive exercises. That does not mean that you ignore what is not so good. But first and foremost you identify what you do right and well.

If you have been struggling with the organising and some of the prioritising of decisions around making one-to-one time possible, this might get a little easier around now. It may become psychologically easier for you to decide to drop some other activities and make new priority time available.

These sorts of judgements become easier as the person picks up a little and starts to show visible progress – blossoms, if you like. You can allow yourself to be impressed with yourselves and how simple it was to achieve this progress with a very natural, simple technique.

If you are an Intensive Interaction 'hero' of any sort and you have been having your try-outs in a 'solo' fashion, this period might be a good time for gently introducing new members of staff to what is taking place.

For the moment keep going with these watch words:

Repetition

Tempo

Pauses, watching and waiting, give the person processing time

Learn to be deft – do not do too much within the activity

Regularly and frequently available

Look for and record all little developments (see Chapter 7)

Getting the 'feel thing'

We can describe the elements of technique for Intensive Interaction and set them out as we are doing here. Nonetheless, we cannot tell you completely about how to do Intensive Interaction.

 Some people are such natural Intensive Interaction practitioners that they seem to have this 'feel' thing as part of their make-up or personality. There were several members of staff in the team during the development and first research projects of the 1980s who could be described like this. It was very useful to watch them working and be analytical about their style.

Much of the technique is an intuitive 'feel' for how to apply the approach. This will usually come relatively quickly as you start to observe that you are having a positive effect on the other person. You gradually become very naturally comfortable with being an Intensive Interaction practitioner.

You could usually see two main elements of their 'naturalness'. First, they were very good at tuning-in and picking up tiny bits of feedback from the other person. Second, they just seemed to know how to avoid doing too much with their own behaviour – a natural sense of minimalism and of getting their behaviour just right.

How do Intensive Interaction activities end?

This is a frequently asked question during courses. It is an issue because, of course, an Intensive Interaction activity can be any sort of length, just like any conversation. They can be 20 seconds; they can be 20 minutes.

The activities finish in a variety of ways. Mostly they fizzle out as the learning person has enough. This is possibly the best ending. You learn to recognise the first stages of the other person getting there by reading their behaviour and responses. You will then quite naturally 'taper-off' or 'fizzle-out' your input so that the whole thing gradually slows down and stops. Mostly in the early stages this happens quickly.

Mostly, but not always (for example, Ferdi, 'Let's go'), the activities are naturally short for a person in the early stages.

It is a good idea, if you try and avoid sudden, abrupt finishes to activities. It is better usually if they wind down smoothly, especially if the person goes to quite a higher level of arousal during the activity. However, some people you work with can prefer this sort of ending, for instance, suddenly standing up and walking away without any preamble – 'Thanks, enjoyed that but that's it, ta-ra'.

There can be difficulties, of course, when 'enough' for a person becomes 45 minutes. Therefore you might need to start finding out how to end the activities by using the intentional 'fizzling-out' described above. Depending on the person's understanding you might even start verbally preparing her or him during the activity. You can even try some sort of countdown. This could be verbal or visual.

The person gets very excited, the activity can get out of control

Communication is exciting is it not? People at early levels of development can be 'raw' and the newly found interest and thrill can be a little too much for them.

They might have difficulty handling the happiness and the emotions. The new sense of connection with other people could be provoking them into new levels of gladness but, unfortunately, that high arousal might be difficult for them to deal with.

Figure 5.4 helps us think about some of this. The diagram is first and foremost a tool for thinking through challenging situations. However, it helps us to think about how people can get too excited in the early stages of doing Intensive Interaction activities.

The activities will probably, mostly, take everybody 'up' in arousal. This is a good thing. Life and all daily experience are a variety of textures. Indeed, for many people, it may be the case that going up in arousal helps them to take part in the activities. Many people seem to 'switch-on' better as communicators when they go up somewhat in emotional and psychological arousal.

However, the people we work with are people who are at early levels of development and they can be unskilled or even inexperienced in the art of dealing with and controlling their own arousal levels. They can go too high during the interaction and the results can be some difficult and undesirable behaviours.

Actually, that is another reason why it is such a good idea for them to be doing Intensive Interaction activities. They have an opportunity, regularly, to rehearse going up in arousal and coming down again under some control. They carry out this rehearsal in partnership with a more experienced person who is already good at it.

Indeed, go back to Chapter 2, 'What does Intensive Interaction teach?'. One of the outcomes listed under the 'fundamentals of communication' is 'learning to regulate and control arousal levels'. This learning is a predicted, foreseen aspect of Intensive

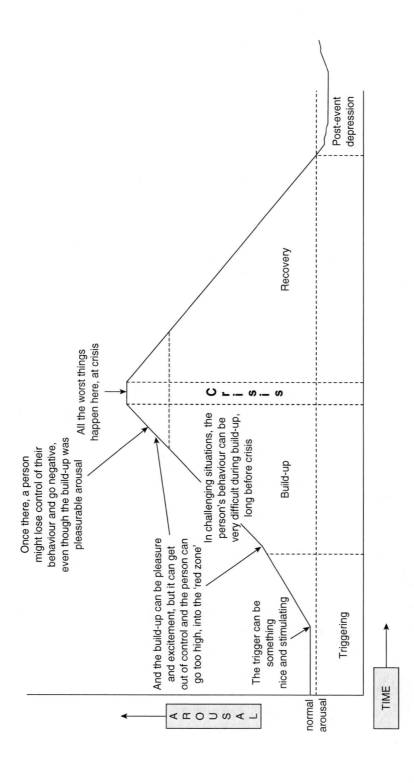

Figure 5.4 The stages of a violent/difficult incident
Based on Arnett, A. and Hewett, D. (1994) 'Safety first: violent and aggressive behaviour: principles for managing difficult situations,' *Community Care*, 10 March.

Labels within figure:

AROUSAL

TIME

normal arousal

Triggering

The trigger can be something nice and stimulating

Build-up

In challenging situations, the person's behaviour can be very difficult during build-up, long before crisis

And the build-up can be pleasure and excitement, but it can get out of control and the person can go too high, into the 'red zone'

Once there, a person might lose control of their behaviour and go negative, even though the build-up was pleasurable arousal

All the worst things happen here, at crisis

Crisis

Recovery

Post-event depression

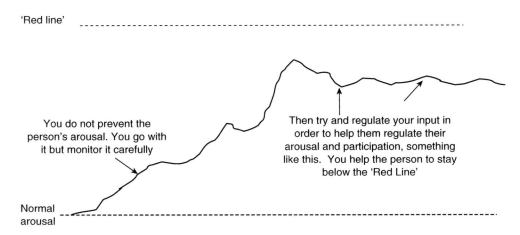

Figure 5.5 Regulating arousal levels during interaction

Interaction activities, just as with the early learning of parent–infant interaction. The person carries out this learning in real-life, active and dynamic partnership situations.

However, if the person you are interacting with frequently becomes uncontrollably excited, there are two options to try:

1. Try the deliberately coming down option – rehearse gradually withdrawing your input in order to fizzle it out, perhaps before the person goes too high.

2. Have frequent, deliberately shorter activities for a while in order to rehearse successful activities that do not go too high – in fact there might be a combination here with deliberately fizzling it out.

Alternatively, or again perhaps in combination with the possibilities above, the idea will be to spend some time consciously focusing on the 'regulating' aspect of the person's participation in the activity.

That does not mean being directive and controlling in any way, more that you stay especially tuned-in to and conscious of, where her or his arousal is going at any given moment.

You do not try and prevent the person from going up in arousal, but you attempt to regulate your input in order to have a regulating effect on their activity. Let us try and put that into a diagram (Figure 5.5) based on Figure 5.4.

Flow and mutuality

'Flow' is a good Intensive Interaction word. Another way of thinking what you are trying to do is that you are trying to establish a sense of flow; a sense of communication flow that is shared with the other person.

At this stage of the activities with the person, you are looking to try to establish a variety of activities that are likely to be productive and give many textures of experience to the person and, yes, hoping for, looking for, the communication learning outcomes, the progress. But it is important to remember that one of the first attainments is for the person to be able to take part in the flow of an activity. To recognise, appreciate and enjoy the fact that they can do it with you and probably your teammates.

It is the most normal but also wonderful thing to have plenty of opportunities daily to enjoy the simple human experience of nattering and chattering for no particular purpose other than the pleasure of it. And through the flow of the experience, there is the joy of being mutual with another person, connected, cooperating, sharing the experience together.

Remember what we wrote in Chapter 1 about the functions of communication for all of us? Our main use of our communication abilities seems to be simply to natter and chatter, with no particular concrete outcome to the experience. We simply enjoy the social connections frequently.

For infants learning to be communicators and for the people we are thinking about here, this is a critical issue. During the regular, natural flow of these nattering and chattering activities, the crucial communication attainments such as those described in 'The fundamentals of communication' are established and developed.

So, let us again remember the simple basics, and you and your colleagues achieve this by:

- tuning-in

- allowing the repetition of what works for the person

- time, tempo, giving the person time and space within the activities to think, process and decide

- pauses that allow the person to process, think, decide, maybe have a rest and then come back to you

- building the flow of the activity jointly with her or him

- therefore, really allowing the activities to flow at a speed that is right for the other person

- the success within this gently dynamic shared situation promotes feelings of power, initiative and connection perhaps for the first time in that person's life

- have these activities frequently, regularly; allow the person plenty of practice day by day.

6

Further and continuing progress

Dave Hewett

This chapter looks at:

- Progress – activities and sessions are working and 'spiralling'

  - Further development and progress feels gradual and seamless
  - Keep doing frequent, regular activities or sessions
  - Carry on enjoying everything
  - Natural momentum
  - Repetition and Repertoire
  - Spill-over and 'Interactivity'
  - Ways of developing variety
  - Spiralling

- Recognising progress outcomes

  - Types of progress
  - Feeling comfortable with 'emergence'

- Mid- to long-term possibilities

  - The person is absolutely flying with progress and development. It occurs so quickly and naturally it is difficult to keep track
  - Progression seems slow and painstaking, but we are realistic and we know where we are
  - We seemed to be doing really well with her or him for quite a while, but now we are just in a rut
  - Everything is progressing quite well, you can appreciate the sense of natural momentum and gradual achievements
  - She or he is starting to be involved in more speech and language exchanges
  - She or he is starting to do and get involved in all sorts of things

- Ultimately, how far will they go?

Progress – activities and sessions are working and 'spiralling'

Further development and progress feels gradual and seamless

Once again let us emphasise that any sense of a sequence of 'stages' here in our description is for the sake of dividing the book into a manageable structure. That is true even when we sometimes write phrases such as 'at this stage'. Therefore, at this stage of your Intensive Interaction work, there should not be any sense of passing from one clear stage to another. In fact it should all feel seamless, gradual and whole.

So, things are getting going. You have established activities that start up most of the time without too much difficulty. There might be a range of different types of interaction activity with the person and/or the sense that the range is gently developing and extending.

 Starting Intensive Interaction work with a person who is already somewhat social and communicative

For many of you reading this book, your starting point for Intensive Interaction activities might seem to be somewhere within this section – you are not starting from 'scratch' with a person who is withdrawn from contact and difficult to reach.

You are working with a person who is already social in various ways, maybe even easy to be with, yet you know that her or his communication abilities could and should be much more developed and sophisticated.

So your work with that person is more about picking up from where you are at with her or him and doing positive things to move them on and extend their range of abilities and knowledge. You should find plenty of advice in this section as to how to go about this. But as we mentioned before, we would also still advise reading the previous section.

The priorities outlined in the next six sections are fairly simple:

• Keep doing what you are doing, and feel and enjoy the sense of 'flow'.

• Recognise and allow for the developing sense of enjoyable, natural momentum.

• Recognise, record and celebrate progress.

Keep on doing frequent, regular activities or sessions

So, as always, the first priority in making forward progress with the person is to maintain the frequent activities and the sense of flow within the activities and within the Intensive Interaction work as a whole. Continue to organise plenty of one-to-one times each day with the members of staff who are the main interaction partners for the person.

There should be a nicely occurring sense of natural momentum – the activities and the communication routines have their own 'life'. When it is going well, it is almost not an effort to have the activities in any sense. It is pleasurable, successful and rewarding for everybody involved.

Continue to work hard on the observations and recording of the person's progress outcomes. This is a state of mind for a staff team just as much as it is an administrative procedure. Try to view the record-keeping as exciting. Each little new thing the person does is part of your reward for your clever work and effort. Try to be 'buzzed-up' and alive and alert for spotting all these new developments in your person's life.

The record-keeping becomes more and more important over long periods of time. The activities should be enjoyably repetitive, but yes, repetitive. For some people their progress is genuinely slow and might remain in the realm of tiny little advances week by week. It is vital to maintain the observations in order for the team to recognise that the input is achieving the forward progress.

However, see the discussion later in this chapter. We need to remember also, that for some people, big progress is probably not a realistic prospect, perhaps due to their age at the time of starting Intensive Interaction work, or to the nature of their impairment. For them, we need to recognise that having Intensive Interaction is simply the way of communicating and relating that works for them. Therefore, simply having it available in their lives, for the rest of their lives, as their way of connecting and having social contact, is the aim and the outcome of the activities for them.

Carry on enjoying everything

Do not forget that the first imperative in all Intensive Interaction work is that it is enjoyable – for both people. Most teams and members of staff comment that when they have a sensation of 'lift-off' with a person, it is not difficult to be motivated to have the activities. It is easier to be with the person generally and there is the sensation that you can actually have a 'conversation' with them. In fact, in a sense, it is a good thing for members of staff to be motivated simply to have chitter-chatter time with the person. This can be a more human, more effective motivation than 'activating sessions in order to achieve progress'.

 Notes from a research project

'Very calm and still. Felt very warm and pleasurable for me. Very close feelings you get when the student is quiet with you.'

(Elena)

'I felt really connected with P. for the first time – it felt like real interaction.'

(Tony)

'Best levels of mutual pleasure yet … I felt on a real high.'

(Bella)

> 'Didn't want to stop interacting as I was having a good session ...'
>
> (Deepti)
>
> 'It felt great, it was brilliant, felt as if J. was really enjoying my company.'
>
> (Louisa)

It is so important that you do not have any doubts about this aspect of Intensive Interaction work. It is right for you to expect to enjoy individual activities with your person, to enjoy the whole process. It is right for you to have the human expectation that the other person has the ability to give you pleasure and fulfilment. This is how the system of communication learning works.

We have included a few quotes to help you with this area of thinking. They are there because in this day and age it can almost seem like some members of staff and teams can experience a sort of guilt if they are enjoying themselves at work, and enabling their pupils or service users to have enjoyment for much of the day.

However, around this time of the process of developing the activities there can gradually be the start of some dissatisfaction. You may start to re-evaluate other things done with the person that take up time that could be dedicated to Intensive Interaction.

If you are a new Intensive Interaction practitioner or team, also around this time you may start to think about broadening your work. You may have been going carefully so far, taking it easy on yourself, taking our advice not to overwhelm yourself with the number of people you are working with.

 Technique point: start broadening your experience

With each new person you work with, you learn more about how to interact with all the people you have been interacting with so far.

You further develop that 'feel' for how to do Intensive Interaction as well as the intellectual knowledge.

Perhaps now you may feel some confidence individually and as a team to spread your work out to other people, going with them through the features of Intensive Interaction outlined so far. You will probably find that with each new person you work with, you learn more about how to interact with all the people you have been interacting with so far.

Natural momentum

The first and main element in all of the progress and development that is now to come should be a sense of natural momentum. Things lift-off, continue to lift-off and 'spiral' upwards day by day, almost without you consciously thinking about it.

Do not do things that get in the way of natural momentum

A major issue is that, so often, we like to schedule, control, prescribe and detail our work. This is not necessarily a bad thing.

However, this almost second-nature bureaucratic trend that we have can be a major barrier to the natural momentum of Intensive Interaction development.

The activities work – the other person really enjoys them – she or he wants to do them a lot – you are enjoying doing them – you are doing them more without even really realising it – the person is developing a little – the activities last a little longer – gradually there are variations, and further types of activity develop …

All this often happens in these stages without the practitioner or the team even being fully consciously aware of it. In fact, sometimes the big trick for practitioners is to be aware enough not to do things that get in the way of this natural process.

Repetition and repertoire

We are aware that we keep repeating this, but do not worry about the repetitions. Repetition is the main 'engine room' of forward progress.

Repertoire

Repertoire is a handy Intensive Interaction word used to describe the range of activities that are familiar to and shared by the person who is learning and the interaction partner or partners. It is a word borrowed from musical performance – a musician or a band has a 'repertoire' of pieces they know well and can perform easily.

It is recognised that repetition is important in early learning. In interactions with infants, it is estimated that the main content of nearly all interactions in the early stages is repetition of things that the two people have previously done together.

In most of our general activities and work with our pupils and service users, we probably do not do enough repetition. Not enough enjoyable, positive consolidation of where the learner person is 'at' at this moment in time.

The three 'Rs' of Intensive Interaction

So, another gimmicky way of thinking about doing Intensive Interaction is that it has three 'Rs':

Responsiveness
Repetition
Repertoire.

Sometimes it feels like we are trying to move on maybe before the person has benefited fully from where they are 'at' and has spent enough at this place in order to be ready to be moving on to the next 'stage'. We often have a work culture (particularly in schools) where we are desperately striving to move on to the next 'stage' – as quickly as possible.

For the person who is learning about the complexities of being a communicator, repetition gives:

familiarity
predictability
a sense of safety and security
a sense of control and expertise

By now you will have already built up a 'repertoire' of activities that are the mainstream of what your person enjoys doing with you and other members of staff. You might be able to identify within the activities the way in which the repetition also makes a firm and safe base for variations, divergences and experimentations with new things within the activities. Again, this is usually something like a gradual, natural process and you may not notice that it is happening until you stop and think about it.

Spillover and 'interactivity'

As activities develop and there is a sensation of 'momentum' becoming established, you might also notice what we can call 'spillover' from the activities. That means that things that have been established within the specific Intensive Interaction activities, start to occur at other times and in other contexts.

This might start happening without you even noticing it at first, because interacting in this way becomes so normal and natural, unremarkable. The exchange of vocalisations established during Intensive Interaction becomes the happy exchange during mealtimes, the hand-patting, turn-taking exchange happens while walking along the corridor, or in the living room.

There are many possibilities, of course, and these developments are to be welcomed and celebrated. Please, also try to recognise them well enough to record them as progress outcomes! It would usually mean that the person's growing sense of communication awareness is starting to show in everything she or he does.

Case Study: *Spillover*

The first properly established activity with Gerhardt took place in the sensory room. He enjoyed tapping on one of the light panels and having his tapping imitated by the member of staff with him.

Within the sensory room, this generalised to the radiator and the door – he would use these too for the tapping game.

One evening in the lounge, Siobhan noticed that Gerhardt had slid a few feet across the floor to be near the radiator. It took her a few moments to realise that he was tapping on it, and a further few moments for her to realise the significance of what was taking place.

As we have written, it is a good thing always to maintain the habit of setting aside one-to-one time for that person frequently and regularly. However, over time and with the person's growing and advancing powers, it may be that it is all of the 5- and 10-second little communication moments that start occurring that are as significant as the big, set-piece sessions.

So look for little activities and moments that support the main activities, for example:

- remembering to do 5-second contacts in passing

- having non-verbal moments – eye contact and facial expression contacts even from across the room

- staying tuned-in around the person generally – listening for potentially initiating vocalisations

- watching out for anything the person does that may be new, general communication

- remember to start using *your* interactive awareness in the way you conduct all activities with the person.

Technique point: your 'interactiveness'

Remember not to leave your 'interactiveness' behind in the Intensive Interaction 'session'.

Take it with you everywhere, have it switched on in everything you do.

You are gradually working towards Intensive Interaction – and everything that develops from its use – just being the normal, natural social environment for the person and for the other people where you work.

When we wrote the first book on Intensive Interaction in 1994, we invented a word. We described this gradual process of Intensive Interaction activities spilling over into the general rhythm of the day and gradually changing the way we did things, as 'interactivity'.

'Interactivity'

We are not sure if the term 'interactivity' is a grammatically correct one, but we find it useful shorthand to describe a concept. This is a term we developed and used casually at Harperbury School. What we mean by 'interactivity' is as follows. When we were developing our work on these principles, we first thought about the interaction sequences as a special, intense activity which happened at a particular time of the day. We then got on with all the other activities which made up the working day and which were long established. We found some developments occurring naturally however.

First, some students quickly made progress to the point where they were starting to initiate – to look for and ask for interactions. Inconveniently, this would happen incidentally at any time, not just when it was timetabled. We realised quickly that the best thing to do was to be flexible enough to respond to the learner's initiations wherever and whenever possible. It was, after all, an important part of the learning that we respond to their voluntary attempts at communicating. This had the effect on us that we were starting to hold ourselves ready in 'interaction mode' throughout the day. This had the further effect of starting to reduce emphasis on our previous style of doing things. We were starting to change our style of working generally, moving more and more away from being dominating, controlling, forceful.

At the same time, the more we took part in the set-piece interaction sequences, the more we thought about and discussed the power and significance of this way of behaving as members of staff. As a natural process, this style of being with the students started to be influential in everything that we did. We started to relax more and become more lighthearted in the way we organised and led any activity. Again, we were becoming less dominant and forceful, using our behaviour to help our students be motivated to participate.

(Melanie Nind and Dave Hewett (1994) *Access to Communication*. London: David Fulton)

There is a big issue here. Even if the understandable starting point for doing Intensive Interaction with a person was carefully scheduled one-to-one time in the sensory room, it must not remain imprisoned in that context. It must break out into the general world.

We can do Intensive Interaction for specific, maybe therapeutic, reasons of course, but it is not just a therapy, it is that person's way of being in the social world; and the social world is everywhere.

For those people with high dependencies, do not forget the one-to-one time that is available when giving care. We tend to think about such people as having profound and multiple learning difficulties but, actually, most of the people we are thinking about in this book need assistance with daily routines at some time.

As we suggested previously, you might already have been exploiting these situations from the start of the Intensive Interaction work. However, it can frequently be the case that the person's growing abilities will be evident during the routines of helping them wash, eat, dress, and so on.

These are one-to-one situations happening frequently that *they* can exploit. It is important therefore in your workplace culture, to do the best you can to avoid 'zipping' through caregiving. Rather, if possible, recognise it fully as quality time, communication time and responsiveness time.

One of the most frequently asked questions about the progress that people can make is something like, 'Will he learn to initiate interactions, to ask for them?'

The answer is of course, yes, almost everybody does. Some people 'get the hang' of things quickly and start to initiate at a very early stage. With others, perhaps moving on more slowly, it is a later development as their powers gradually accumulate.

The ways in which people make the initiations are of course, tremendously varied. It can be as unmissable as her or him grabbing hold of you and physically turning you towards them. It can be as subtle and tiny as a soft, breathy vocalisation or a slightly poked-out tongue with a person who may have very restricted movements.

The practice issue for you, of course, is that not all people will make unmistakable initiations. The ability of others successfully to initiate is dependent upon your and your teammates' ability to have a sort of general, environmental tuned-inness through the day.

Case Study: *John*

I had known John for eight years on the day this happened. For nearly all of that time, John had been a person more or less completely in his own world of rhythmic, self-absorbed behaviour, frequently looking intently at the yellow toy he flapped a few inches from his eyes. In recent months they had been working intensively with him in the project.

I was in the classroom, talking to Elena. A hand came over my shoulder, grasped my chin, quite hard really and jerked my head around. There, 6 inches away, John's eyes were looking directly into mine, softly, intently. It took me more or less the rest of the day to come to terms with my own emotional reaction to that moment.

(Dave Hewett)

Your person's initiations, requests for an interaction, are of course a 'major spillover' from the scheduled activities. Your response to them, your willingness to take them up on their request, is a major aspect of 'interactivity'.

You can anticipate that developing the motivation and the skill to initiate is a major life event for the person you are working with. It is a potentially wonderful moment for them, so it is important that her or his initiations are successful and effective. That will depend on our ability with 'interactivity' and whether we are flexible enough in our practices to have time to respond. But we want the person to be a communicator, an initiator. This cannot always be at times that are convenient for us.

 ### Notes from a research project

'J. simply so different today: saliva noises very loud (invitational?); not rocking very much; looking around more – glancing toward Nikki especially (invitational?)'.

'C. wandered across the class and stood across the table from where I was sat. Stopped and looked directly at me … maintained this eye contact for a few seconds and then laughed.'

If you are a parent reading this and your Intensive Interaction practice is your wonderful way of interacting with your own child in your own home, the issues here are probably not such a problem. In a school classroom, day centre or even a house for people with learning disabilities, there can be all sorts of issues here about workplace organisation. See Chapter 8 for more details.

The biggest difficulty will obviously occur if your workplace is rigidly organised and timetabled. We hope we are making suggestions throughout this book about ways of organising in order to be more flexible for the communication work generally. Indeed, if you are new to Intensive Interaction, you are hopefully reading this section before starting work.

Also, there is one positive tip. Making a positive response in order to ensure that an initiation is successful does not necessarily mean starting up a full-blown session every time. In the school described in 'Notes from a research project', there was a gradual evolution from quite rigid working towards something more flexible. There were two main ways developed for addressing the students' initiations:

1. Becoming more flexible generally, working slower, having more communication time within and throughout everything that was happening.

2. Practising the art of the 20-second 'No sorry, not right now', so that even while 'No' is the answer, the initiation is still successful, still received a response.

Ways of developing variety

With many people in the early stages, there may not be a wide variety in the repertoire of activities. Indeed, with some people the repertoire may remain limited for a long time before it starts branching out.

Remember what we wrote in Chapter 5: just because the interactions remain 'samey' and do not seem to develop much variety in the activities, this does not necessarily mean that there is no progress. There can be all sorts of progress occurring for the person's performance *within* these activities.

In any event, up until now, the first emphasis is on getting the activities working, established, happening easily, regularly and frequently. Then, as we have stressed here, the second priority is the sense of natural momentum and spiralling. Nonetheless, it is a reasonable expectation that as the variety of activities expands, so does the variety of opportunities for the learning to continue to branch out. In Figure 6.1 we list some ideas for creating more variation in the activities that make up the interactions. Go carefully with these suggestions and do not do too many of them all at once. In fact, the best advice is to try them one at a time so that you are clear about what happened when one of them works.

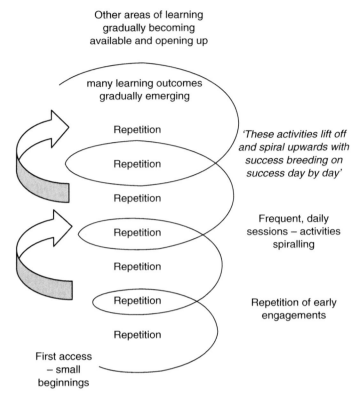

Figure 6.1   The 'spiral' of progress and development

 Technique point: suggestions for increasing variety in the repertoire

- Do some more observations of your person and of colleagues interacting with her or him. Think about other, further things that the person is doing that provide opportunities for responding, but which at present you do not use those behaviours or aspects of the person.
- Is any one person in the team getting a lot more happening than everyone else? What is it that she or he is doing?
- Sensitively try making your own gentle variations in the way that you take part in the repertoire activities. Stay alert for whether this immediately provides the possibility of something new happening.
- Try doing some gentle 'teasing', following the usual games, but sometimes slowing down or holding back in order to 'enjoyably provoke' the other person into new actions. In Australia, Mark Barber and colleagues term this 'sabotage'.
- Consider arranging for a completely different member of staff to join in sometimes. This new personality may bring a different dimension.
- Have varieties of objects or things readily available near to where you are having the interactions. The other person may choose to bring one of those things in.
- Consider and plan carefully crafted initiations of something new using Scenario 2 – be careful not to get stuck and get insistent if it does not work.
- Consider and evaluate (positively!) your own style (using video helps). Are you:

  - missing anything during the interactions that could be a new variation?
  - perhaps visibly doing a bit too much and diminishing the time and space available to the other person for thinking and creativity?
  - maybe not being responsive enough sometimes – for example, to vocalisations?

Spiralling

Here is a practical theory which is generally helpful in thinking about how progress occurs for a person. We have used the word 'spiral' a few times so far. In this section we will give more detail on the use of this word. Hopefully, you should find it really helpful as a way of thinking about how the Intensive Interaction work continues to progress and develop with a person over time. Two diagrams help to explain what we mean (Figures 6.1 and 6.2).

'Spiralling' is a word often used in all sorts of ways in order to think about how things develop and progress. It has been used sometimes in the parent–infant interaction research literature to describe the way in which an infant's communication knowledge and performance gradually grows in partnership with adults.

One of the good things about the 'spiral' for us, is that it helps us to visualise communication development as *not* happening in a straight line, or in a nice, tidy sequence. The concept is borrowed from some of the parent–infant interaction research studies. The sense of the activities spiralling is an image for the natural momentum and the repetition.

Figures 6.1 and 6.2 also help us to visualise the 'process-central' nature of Intensive Interaction work. As is now probably clear from your own experiences, in this way of working, the emphasis is on regularly and frequently activating the processes of the activities. It is not on the setting and working towards objectives.

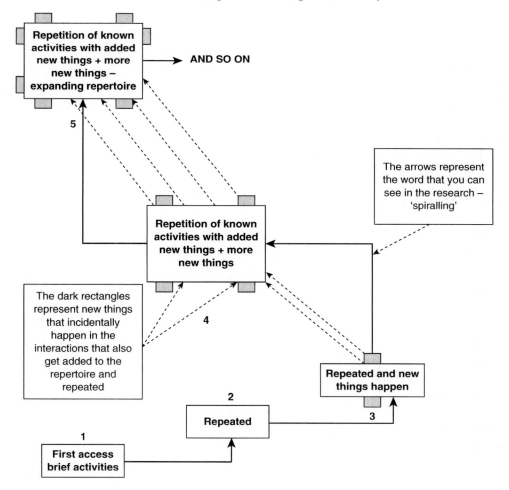

Figure 6.2 The activities lift-off and spiral upwards day by day

Recognising progress outcomes

It is so important to monitor and keep track of the person's progress. This is a demand of your standard practice in most services, for all sorts of good reasons. However, we have also emphasised how important it is for you the practitioner, to give yourself good feedback that your work is achieving results.

We would say the same to parents and family members who are not working in services. We do not like to suggest that you start doing record-keeping and administration of what is essentially family life. However, the giving yourself feedback issue can apply for you as well.

Also, of course, for some people, progress can be slow and gradual. If you do not keep track of it in reasonable detail, you could lose touch with the fact that progress is being made.

Chapter 7 provides you with advice on approaches to record-keeping and tracking. This section is more about how being aware of the progress will feed into the sense of natural momentum of activities.

 Bethany

Here is an example of a teacher looking for the most subtle signals of mutuality from a young woman with the most profound nature of disability.

'We have learnt that after being hoisted onto or close to the adult working with her, it is noticeable that Bethany's body and therefore her breathing relaxes after approximately five minutes. There is then a sensation that she "tunes-in" to you.'

Julia Rhodes in Rhodes, J. and Hewett, D. (2010) 'The human touch: physical contact and making a social world available for the most profoundly disabled.'

PMLD Link, 22 (2): 11–14.

Types of progress

From the very first moment of starting to try out Intensive Interaction with a person, it is important to remember that tiny can be big. Sometimes tiny new things the person does can be, or be the sign of, significant new progress. This can particularly be the case with people who have the most severe multiple disabilities.

For this reason, it can be so important to shoot videos of what you are doing with the person and to evaluate the video footage.

Try to remember, also, that the progress outcomes will not be revealed only within the Intensive Interaction activities. They can occur within, and be related to, all aspects of their daily experience. So we can say that the progress outcomes can be in two main areas:

- purely communication developments

- well-being and developments in all areas of life.

Figure 6.3 illustrates these two areas of possibility in more detail.

Feeling comfortable with 'emergence'

Another reason for the importance of observations of progress and record-keeping is that the progress outcomes are 'emergent'. By this we mean the progress outcomes arise or emerge over time as a result of the process. The process is the regular, frequent activation of Intensive Interaction activities. That is why repertoire and repetition are important. This is how the whole thing operates for developing infants in the 'natural model'. They learn the complicated communication attainments within an enjoyable *process* of repeated activities.

The learning outcomes – particularly communication abilities, but as we shall see, many things – emerge and arise gradually. They come about as a result of the process of doing the activities.

So progress with Intensive Interaction will be gradual over time, various periods of time – different periods of time for each individual person. Some people make progress quite quickly, others much more slowly. So it is important to feel comfortable with this idea that the outcomes emerge gradually as a result of the person being in the process.

Most of our work is not like that. Mostly we work in a way where we set objectives or targets beforehand. Then the activities we do with a person drive towards the objective. This is a satisfactory way of working for various things, but Intensive Interaction does not work like that. Intensive Interaction is a process.

Then, two important further issues need to be kept in mind as the Intensive Interaction work progresses:

1. Although Intensive Interaction is an approach borrowed from observations of natural human learning, the people we are working with are not likely to make progress as quickly as infants in the 'natural' model.

2. Any person's progress is unlikely to be smooth and continuous all of the time.

If you looked at it on a graph, a person's progress is unlikely to be like that in Figure 6.4, but is likely to be more like that in Figure 6.5.

People do not make progress and develop in straight lines. It would be lovely if they did, but they do not. Even with developing infants, it is recognised that they do not make continuous progress. They have lulls, like the plateaus in Figure 6.5.

It is assumed that there are periods of time where the brain does not want to take anything more in, but rather to work with what has just been taken in. For the people with whom we are working, these plateaus can last for quite some time.

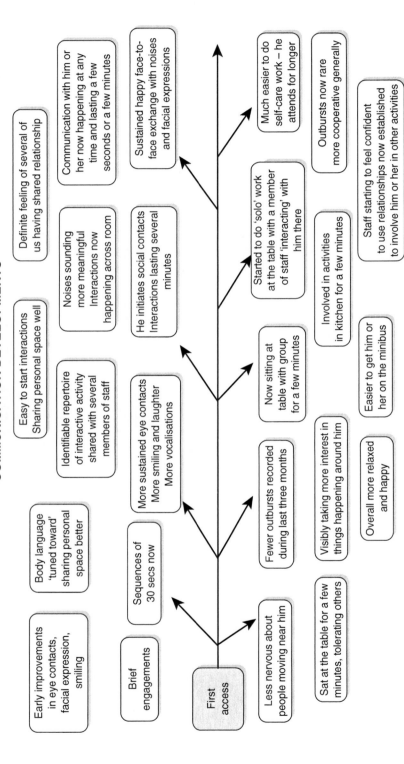

COMMUNICATION DEVELOPMENTS

Early improvements in eye contacts, facial expression, smiling

Body language 'tuned toward' sharing personal space better

Easy to start interactions
Sharing personal space well

Definite feeling of several of us having shared relationship

Identifiable repertoire of interactive activity shared with several members of staff

Noises sounding more meaningful
Interactions now happening across room

Communication with him or her now happening at any time and lasting a few seconds or a few minutes

Brief engagements

Sequences of 30 secs now

More sustained eye contacts
More smiling and laughter
More vocalisations

He initiates social contacts
Interactions lasting several minutes

Sustained happy face-to-face exchange with noises and facial expressions

First access

Less nervous about people moving near him

Sat at the table for a few minutes, tolerating others

Fewer outbursts recorded during last three months

Visibly taking more interest in things happening around him

Overall more relaxed and happy

Now sitting at table with group for a few minutes

Easier to get him or her on the minibus

Involved in activities in kitchen for a few minutes

Started to do 'solo' work at the table with a member of staff 'interacting' with him there

Staff starting to feel confident to use relationships now established to involve him or her in other activities

Much easier to do self-care work – he attends for longer

Outbursts now rare
more cooperative generally

DEVELOPMENTS IN OTHER AREAS

Figure 6.3 Communication developments/developments in other areas

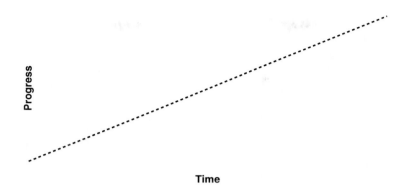

Figure 6.4 Theoretical progress diagram

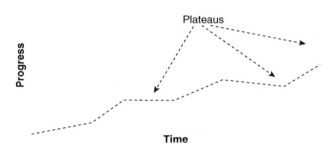

Figure 6.5 Actual progress diagram

Mid- to long-term possibilities

Time passes. You may be a year or two down the line from the start point. There is a range of possible experiences that practitioners and teams describe as they move into the long-term establishment of Intensive Interaction activities:

- Wow, our person is still absolutely flying with progress and development.

- Progression in every regard is slow and painstaking, but we know where we are and we are realistic.

- We seemed to be doing really well with her or him for quite a while, but now we are just in a rut. We do the same things over and over and there is no further progress.

- Everything is progressing quite well; you can appreciate the sense of natural momentum and gradual achievement.

- She or he is starting to do and get involved in all sorts of things.

Let us deal with each of these in turn.

The person is absolutely flying with progress and development. It occurs so quickly and naturally it is difficult to keep track

This is not the most usual scenario, but it does happen and you should try not to be too surprised by it if this is one of your experiences.

Some people can present as being extremely difficult to reach – they can look difficult to reach, isolated in their own world of rhythmic self-stimulation perhaps. But, when you get their immediate social world just right for them, it can turn out that this person was not difficult to reach at all. She or he only *looked* difficult to reach.

In reality, this was a person who was sort of cognitively 'primed' and 'raring to go', simply needing the correct social world to be made available to her or him. The correct 'social world' is likely to be sensitive people around her or him who are armed with Intensive Interaction processes.

This scenario is most likely to occur with some children in early years, who, when given the opportunity, take off and make rapid progress. It seems as if they had been 'stalled' at first, waiting for the right input.

Indeed, sometimes we can have the uncomfortable realisation that a person's lack of progress is more to do with us not doing the right things with them than with their level of impairment. This difficult realisation can particularly occur when it is an older person, even an adult, who at last gets going and flies with progress and development when you get things right.

Advice:

- It sounds obvious, daft even, but do try not to do anything that will get in the way of your person's progress.

- Better still, really sit down together and make sure that you know, that you can identify everything you are doing that is positively contributing to the progress. This will include:

  - the Intensive Interaction work
  - other positive experiences that are 'outside' the Intensive Interaction work, particularly nurturing, 'feel good' experiences that occur regularly for the person
  - an overall sense of the atmosphere that the person is experiencing – you are probably working in a beneficial way – what is the team style? What are its elements? If someone asks you, 'How are you achieving that?', can you describe the team processes and working principles?
  - all other learning opportunities.

- Keep doing what you are doing.

Progression seems slow and painstaking, but we are realistic and we know where we are

Progress can be many different things across the range of people we are working for in this book. As we have observed, some people have far-reaching cognitive impairments that will inevitably be a major factor in their progress and development. This would likely include people with more profound multiple impairments and people whose impairments are so extensive they may be able to show few responses.

Case Study: *An available social world*

In the previous example of the work being carried out with Bethany, Julia reported that there was the possibility of some little progress happening. She also talked about the main issue being to continue to do everything they possibly could to make sure that Bethany had an emotionally supportive and understandable social environment available to her.

They realised that the best and only way to be in constant social contact was to be giving Bethany physical contact for as much of the day as possible.

There are also people who do not fit into the above descriptions and who in many ways might be quite active and alert in their lifestyle. Yet their progress with communication can be very slow. Of course, we do not understand everything about the brain, about the nature of impairments and the possible effects of life experiences on a person's motivation.

So, on the one hand, you need to have a sense of realism about the nature of the person's abilities, likely development and lifestyle. Then don't beat yourself up because her/his progress is 'slow' and 'painstaking'. Perhaps it isn't.

On the other hand of course, as a team, beware sinking into a rut of low expectations and low motivation to move on.

Advice:

- Detail, detail, detail. Keep tracking, doing detailed record-keeping with the sorts of observations where you celebrate the 'tiny' bits of progress as big progress for that person.

- Do monthly 'round-ups' of progress as a matter of routine – keep yourself positively informed that though slow, it is there.

- Gently try out new aspects to the interactions (see previous, 'Technique point: suggestions for increasing variety in the repertoire').

- Once again, this is always part of the advice. Use videos to evaluate activities, especially to see if you are missing anything.

Best of all, keep asking yourself if the other person is having a good life because of what you and your colleagues are doing. As we discuss in the next section, for some people, it is vital to have people around them who can offer such responsive interactions. For some, it may be the best thing in their life, for the rest of their life.

We seemed to be doing really well with her or him for quite a while, but now we are just in a rut

Much of the advice that can be given here has been offered also in the previous section. The main thing to think about, though, is something like, 'Is there really, truly no ongoing progress?' Or could it be that we have let our observations and tracking slip over time, with a spiralling down effect on our motivation?

Suggestions:

- Be glad about what you have achieved, go back to your records about how the person was at the start and remind yourself where you are now by comparison to the start point.

- Remember that her or his progress as a communicator does not necessarily need to be continuous and constant. Is she or he happy in the social world that is shared with all of you?

- Shoot and evaluate some video clips of interaction sequences to try to see if you are missing anything.

- If you can organise it, try bringing in one or two 'new faces' to the interactive work with your person. This may bring a different angle, some new, fresh energy.

Everything is progressing quite well; you can appreciate the sense of natural momentum and gradual achievements

If this is your scenario by this stage, you should be enjoying a lovely situation with the person where there is a sensation of overall positivity, with everything 'on the up'. The usual features of good progress over the medium term would be, for instance:

- frequent, easily commenced 'big' interaction activities every day

- the person initiates interaction regularly and is just socially 'in contact' with you throughout the day

- the activities can last for a long time and in fact you are increasingly addressing the need to suggest terminating them owing to your needs to move on to something else

- there are many incidental activities all through the day

- she or he is probably showing all sorts of developments in life generally

- the person's communication abilities are developing and expanding.

She or he is starting to be involved in more speech and language exchanges

We do not understand the reasons why some people seem to progress smoothly to some speech and language facility, some do not and some, especially some people with ASD, quickly learn to use 50 words or so, then no more.

Increased vocalising and a gradual transition to some speech should, logically, be a natural aspect of the flow of the process. However, some further advice is offered in the list below for you to do some more, perhaps deliberate, thinking about promoting further developments in this area:

- It is best to have always been doing this – but be extra vigilant to respond to *all* vocalisations from the person.

- Make a judgement to deliberately use more responses involving running commentary.

- Use running commentary (carefully – do not bombard) that gradually names and brings in things that are happening within and around the interaction at that moment.

- If your person produces a vocalisation that sounds to you like a word, respond (even questioningly) with that word – *Her or him:* 'eeaghhh …', *You:* 'Yeah?' 'Yeah …'

- Be ready to absolutely go with and expand happy vocal turn-taking activities – yes, it might get a little loud.

- Start to accurately tune into the pitch/tone and frequency of the vocalisations/sounds that your partner makes and reflect them back to help with that unique part of the connection.

- Use sounds that are the early precursors to words that carry meaning and may be part of your playful activity such as 'Oh-oh!' 'Splash!' 'Pop!' 'Crash!' 'Slap!'

- Look for and encourage pointing gestures.

- Start to do other games like making silly noises that go with pulling silly faces while looking in the mirror together (yes, with adults too).

She or he is starting to do and get involved in all sorts of things

Another major aspect of the gradual progress is the sense of the person's abilities and activities 'branching out'. The image of 'branching out' is vivid – we can visualise the 'tree of progress.'

We need to remember the pathway that we are on with communication development for a person. When we work on the person's communication ability, we are not only working on communication abilities. We are working towards the person achieving, or at least, having available, everything else in life.

If we visualise this image of the tree (Figure 6.6), learning the ability to communicate and relate is the root formation, with communication then being the trunk that supports all other performances and attainments.

There is a fairly frequent question, 'Well, he's doing very well with communication and has really come on, what's next?' Part of the answer to that is simply, 'Everything else'.

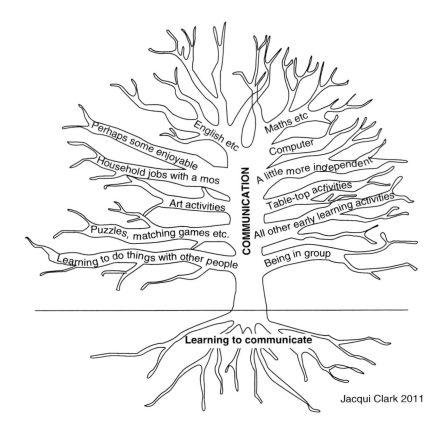

Figure 6.6   Communication tree

Again, caution here, we would always advise not pushing people too hard as they progress in the (still) early stages. However, do look out for this branching out of their abilities and outlook. Look for opportunities to introduce them and involve them in everything else that life has to offer. However this does not mean reducing emphasis on the communication work.

Ultimately, how far will the person go?

When working with Intensive Interaction, it is mostly not possible to be working with a vision of the end-points that we are working towards with the person. Of course, it is highly desirable that they will all become full communicators, full speech and language users. At present, it is not possible to state that this has happened with any person.

However, many people have attained some speech and language use, some a fair amount. Again, we are careful here, since so many practitioners and parents see the attainment of speech as what communication is all about. We hope we have described that desirable as these attainments are, communication is a splendid, many faceted thing.

The ultimate answer to the question above is that we are still finding out how far up the 'spiral' of progression and development any individual may go. However, we have seen that with virtually every person, Intensive Interaction activities bring life enhancing or life transforming access to the social world.

Further reading 📖

If you would like to read about 'emergent outcomes' 'spiralling' and 'process approaches' in further technical detail, try:

'What is Intensive Interaction? Curriculum, process and approach', by Dave Hewett

'Interactive approaches to teaching and learning', by Penny Lacey

both in Hewett, D. (ed.) (2011) *Intensive Interaction: Theoretical Perspectives*. London: Sage.

7

Recording the activities and maintaining the processes

Mark Barber

This chapter looks at:

- **Observation and recording**
- **Observation**
- **Recording what you are doing**
  - **Short term: what to record**
  - **What is the point?**
  - **Medium term**
  - **Long term**
  - **Finally – the 'handover' record**
- **Recording using video**
  - **What sort of camera?**
  - **Other considerations**
  - **Using the camera: brief considerations**
  - **Practical issues**
  - **Does my bum look big?**
  - **Storage**
  - **Saving files**
- **Using video evidence**
  - **Using video as evidence of learning and progress**
  - **Framework for recognising progress**
- **Using video evidence to encourage colleagues**
- **Good luck.**

Observation and recording

Paperwork and keeping a record of what we are doing are invariably the things we all blame for getting in the way of us being able to do more valuable things.

Actually, of course, good records can be really valuable in the long run – and, let us face it, many of us are working with our students and clients for many years.

This chapter focuses on ways to record what you are doing and how you might identify and record the progress or the changes in how the people you work with respond to you and learn about communicating and being social. We also look at how you and your team might take stock of how you have developed as practitioners. Finally, we look at using video and how it can be used as evidence as well as a record of achievement without it becoming too onerous a task.

Observation

Once you have noticed that a person you work with is socially isolated or has difficulty communicating in social situations you should consider Intensive Interaction as an approach to support them. Remember that many of the contacts that people with complex intellectual disabilities experience, are the sort that require them to conform or respond to a request. So, bear in mind that simply approaching the person directly might not be the best way of starting. For the person you are going to support, this looks just like the other sorts of exchanges they have with those around them. So before you approach them, you should take some time to observe them.

Intensive Interaction has been described as an approach which uses the behaviours a person will recognise as their own, as the basis of a conversation, or to develop two-way dialogue. Many people with complex intellectual disabilities are very socially isolated and they often develop ways of 'listening to themselves' or characteristic mannerisms which are sometimes repeated in pulses or cycles. Before trying to engage the person you are going to start supporting in a conversation, it is really useful to have some ideas about how you are going to use these rhythms and motifs of actions to find a connection with them.

Consider how you are going to attract their attention away from their usual (and often consuming) *solitary* focus, towards you – a *social* focus – or what you are going to do to get on their 'intellectual radar'. This should always be accomplished in a way that makes sense to the person you are working with. Bear in mind that, as often as not, the things that you usually do to strike up a conversation with somebody you already know will probably not work with someone who does not understand words, and who has incredible difficulty making sense of or predicting the things that are happening around them in an interconnected way; this is a conversation *without* words.

So look at what they are doing. She or he is doing it because it makes some sense to them or interests them (otherwise they wouldn't do it). You are looking for common ground – something that the person likes to do and which she or he will be familiar with. It might make no sense to you, for example sifting stones, twiddling thread, making wet mouth-sounds, singing apparently random notes, stomping around a room, touching things rhythmically, and so on.

Find somewhere where you can watch the person being themselves – that is, not when they are having their attention focused by someone else but when they are on their own agenda.

15-minute **OBSERVATION RECORD** of_____ **Date** / / Time _____

ENGAGEMENT Person is engaged with another person/in group/next to group/ alone undirected/with chosen item.
CONTEXT E.g. person is on the mats in the corner of the room/facing wall/rocking/ alone but watching others/engrossed in own game/wandering/stationary standing/ gazing [at what?]
SOUNDS E.g. Is person making sounds as they move? E.g. rhythmic noises/vocal babble/singing/other?
VISION E.g. Where, and at what is the person looking at? Is there eye contact with, or tracking of, others/staff/activities/who?
MOVEMENT E.g. does person move rhythmically, around the same area or person? Does she or he pick up objects or touch people? Are specific objects or TYPES of object of interest, examined, held, retained?
TOUCH E.g. what is touched, is there any pattern in how objects **or** people are greeted, watched, felt, used or played with?
PREFERENCE What does the person spend most of their time doing or seem to most enjoy?
COMMUNICATION Which activities seem to be directed at people, what does the person seem to react to with most interest?
INVOLVEMENT Which behaviours can you imagine joining-in with, what might you do to advertise yourself, or get an invitation to join in?

Figure 7.1   15-minute observation record

Photocopiable:
The Intensive Interaction Handbook © Dave Hewett, Graham Firth, Mark Barber and Tandy Harrison, 2012 (Sage)

Fill in the top six boxes on the form in Figure 7.1 with as much information as you can. You should try to do this three or four times to get an idea of their regular pursuits – the patterns of movement, sound or sensation they enjoy.

Once you have thought about how you might 'reply' to a pattern of behaviour, you are beginning to develop your ideas about possible 'topics of conversation' that you might begin to use when you approach the person. Use this information to fill in the bottom two boxes on the form in Figure 7.1.

When you have some ideas about how to 'answer' them in a way that will encourage a flow or interested glance, you wait and watch for the person to do something you have seen before and considered. Then, when the person pauses, you respond encouragingly, but at a distance they are comfortable with, then pause when you see them resume … (did you notice whether the person glanced at you with interest?).

Important note: It will be very valuable if you take 10 minutes of video showing the learner alone, near people and during exchanges with others, simply as a record of your starting point. These might act as baseline evidence of how they interacted with known friends and staff or to the proximity of other people as well as a record of the habits and cycles or activity they were usually seen to get involved in. I promise, you will be glad you did it in six months' time. See the following sections in this chapter, for advice for using and storing video.

Recording what you are doing

Assuming you have started to respond to something the person is doing and they have shown interest in you by 'glancing at you' or 'smiling' or 'stilling' or giggling or coming over for a closer look, this is important: especially if you are a teacher or someone working with a number of people, but also if you are working in residential services, a parent or simply an interested friend, your ability to recognise progress or notice when you are revisiting or embellishing an old game 'format' will be greatly enhanced if you have some record of what you have done previously.

 A 'format' is a term often used to describe a shared 'game', 'pattern', or 'sequence of response' that evolves over time. Established partners often fall into these formats when they revisit or repeat a motif from a previous encounter – it might be a greeting or simply some sort of reference point that both partners remember and repeat.

How do you know if you have made progress if you cannot compare 'what you do now' with 'what you did when you started' when you are supporting someone to be social? Memory is an unreliable thing and we fall readily into the traps of thinking:

- we have made heaps of progress when actually we have simply come to know someone a lot more closely, or

- we have fallen into monotonous 'set pieces' when actually, interactions have changed a lot, but they have done so very gradually.

Some other reflective practice questions

- What was I aiming for when I did that?
- What exactly did I do?
- Why did I choose that action?
- What did I do next?
- What might I have done differently?
- How successful was it?
- What criteria am I using to judge success?
- Could I have dealt with the situation better?
- How did the client feel about it?
- What sense can I make of this in the light of past experience?
- Has this changed how I might do things in the future?

It is important to have some way of recording what we do, the things we respond to, the places where we interact, the things that interest our interactive partner, the way in which they engage us or, indeed, the things they do to tell us they are finished with us. After all it is not just you who might be trying to support this person.

Being systematic about recording what happens leads you into what are known as 'reflective practices'. These practices are known to be one of the key elements of successful practice because when you record what happened in an encounter, you not only think about the sequence of what happened, but *what was important or significant about what happened.*

Short term: what to record

In a context like a classroom or day centre where you might be with seven or ten people all day, it is just not practical to record every encounter or interaction you might have in a day – if you were to do that, you would be writing for more time than you would be with clients and students. Staff at Bayside Special Developmental School in Melbourne, Australia, have been using Intensive Interaction on a daily basis with their students for eight years and their practices have evolved over that extended time to make recording manageable. I recommend that you consider using the 'best practices' that have been developed there.

Technique point

It is valuable to view an 'Intensive Interaction' with someone as a conversation in which you identify common ground with the learner and support them to explore it and the variations and themes possible within it. If you think about interactions in terms of techniques and responses, you will get a bit wooden in your responses, and fall into simply imitating the actions of your partner.

Conversations involve two people in a constant state of mutual adjustment, where variations and themes merge and emerge between the participants, rather than being simple sequences of 'call' and 'response'. Simply remember to ensure that anything you do is a recognisable form of what your partner is doing.

Your actions should always be
'of' the learner.

The convention that has developed over the years is that every staff member in the room records (at least) one interaction they have with each student in any week, *on paper*. While later we see how an interaction is recorded, it is also recommended that, if you are working with groups of people, you should find a way of ensuring that each person has had some purely social contact during the day or shift. This might be done by something as simple as encouraging each staff member to put a tick on a calendar when they have had some quality time. Why? You would be surprised at the number of people with complex intellectual disabilities who get through a day with no agenda-free social contact at all. This ensures that among all the other things that happen in a day, everyone gets some nourishing social contact from each staff member.

When you are in routine everyday contact with the people you are supporting, not every encounter will be significant. Clearly many of the contacts and interactions we have are functional, brief or incidental and do not actually settle into a form that would be useful to record. But *every* staff member has at least one encounter that is 'nourishing' for the person in any day, so recording the detail of what happened during one of these, in the course of a week, is not too much to expect of yourself. In addition to taking the time to record these, you should always make the time to describe what have become known as '"wow!" moments' or '"wow!" interactions' *every* time they happen.

 Making the time to record: forget the idea that you are not working if you are taking time out to record what happened in an interaction. In educational settings (at least) recording should be considered as part of the educational activity – people with complex intellectual disabilities often do not generate evidence of their learning. The record you make will become a part of their evidence of learning.

How?

To do this we use a recording grid like that in Figure 7.2. Three of these grids can fit on a sheet of A4 paper. The grid is made up of three main spaces. The main concept to bear in mind with this grid is the '5-minute rule'; that is *if it takes more than 5 minutes to fill in, you're doing it wrong.*

Figures 7.3 and 7.4 illustrate a record of what happened during an established game that ended up involving two youngsters. The detail of the interaction is not important, but what is important is the process of reflecting on events and separating *what was important about what happened* for the particular people doing the learning from what happened. You might say the interest is in the processes and communicative 'functions' visited rather than the actual events.

The 'shape' of the game is another way of describing the idea of the 'format'. Yet another way of thinking about the 'format' is that it is a 'learning spiral' or 'gently ritualised sequence' – it is actually the common ground that interactions return to, within which different variations or tangents can be explored. You will no doubt notice that 'set pieces' or 'shapes' begin to emerge in your interactions as interactive relationships become established.

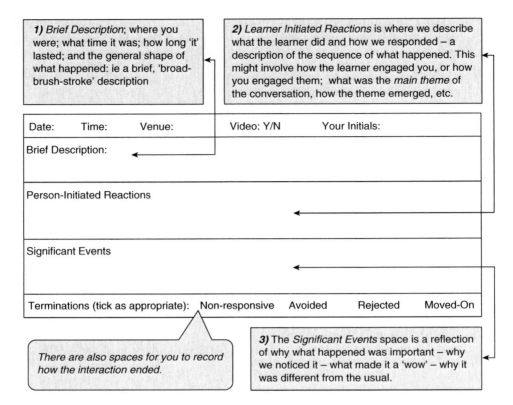

1) *Brief Description*; where you were; what time it was; how long 'it' lasted; and the general shape of what happened: ie a brief, 'broad-brush-stroke' description

2) *Learner Initiated Reactions* is where we describe what the learner did and how we responded – a description of the sequence of what happened. This might involve how the learner engaged you, or how you engaged them; what was the *main theme* of the conversation, how the theme emerged, etc.

Date: Time: Venue:	Video: Y/N Your Initials:
Brief Description:	
Person-Initiated Reactions	
Significant Events	
Terminations (tick as appropriate): Non-responsive Avoided Rejected Moved-On	

There are also spaces for you to record how the interaction ended.

3) The *Significant Events* space is a reflection of why what happened was important – why we noticed it – what made it a 'wow' – why it was different from the usual.

Figure 7.2   Recording grid

Encounter	Date: 30 Aug Time: 10.30 Venue: sensory l/scp Video: N Your Initials: MB
Awareness	**Brief Description:** I positioned myself on the wobbly bridge in the sensory garden to see if Thomas would be interested in joining me and to see if he would revisit/remember the 'bridge wobbling game' – he clearly did
Attention & Response Engagement	**Pupil-Initiated Reactions** He stood next to the wooden slats, joined me in sequences of vocalising, single and multiple stomps on the slats, touching them with his foot [mutual teasing with smiles]. As he eventually defaulted to his treasure [his key ring], I was distracted by Luke and joined him for a couple of minutes – T began to cry into his hand so I rejoined him [immediately stopped crying] – and he rejoined the game of reflecting/adjusting each other's position on the slats. When I was again distracted by LB, he walked across the bridge behind me, vocalising as if in victory that he had got across in spite of me, then standing on the stable bridge pier, he reached for the slats with his toe – watching to see if I reacted. Much hilarity and teasing me with moves to join me on the bridge but actually just keeping me interested in staying with him
Participation Involvement	**Significant Events** • Using 'play' crying to bring me back to him as my focus • Enjoyment of the social game • Adjustment to and prediction of my responses • Keeping me interested by feinting towards doing what he thought I wanted him to do [I think] • Vocal sequences, stomping sequences • It was great to have a situation in which there was a focus and point mutually understood content [I think!!]
	Terminations (tick as appropriate): Non-responsive Avoided Rejected *Moved-On*

Figure 7.3   Illustrative recording grid (1)

	Date: 30 Aug Time: 10.30 Venue: sensory l/scp Video: N Your Initials: MB LUKE
	Brief Description: Luke joined me on the bridge with Thomas and began inviting me to play **his** game by stomping on the bridge and vocalising – when I followed him he led me up the steps of the tower to the slide
Encounter Awareness Attention & Response	**Pupil-Initiated Reactions** When we got to the top of the slide he waved goodbye, but then vocalised and took my hand [?stopping me from leaving him?] … so I helped him on to go down the slide – at the bottom he looked up at me and clapped, vocalising and tapping the bottom of the slide until I followed him – Seeing Thomas upset, I went over to him, but Luke again tried to get me to play with him – by walking into the middle of the bridge and stomping on it – i.e. suggesting the 'shape' of the 'bridge game'. As I attended to Thomas's distress, L continued to vie for me by getting off the bridge and placing his foot on it from the outside and rocking it, laughing and vocalising. When Thomas resumed the game, he joined us with contributions
Engagement Participation	**Significant Events** Competing with another student Joining in – clear invitations, persistence and confirmation and vocalisation to attract & direct my attention, he vocalised to emphasise meaning, maintain and confirm social contacts
Involvement	Terminations (tick as appropriate): Non-responsive Avoided Rejected **_Moved-On_**

Figure 7.4   Illustrative recording grid (2)

While these patterns become largely predictable, it is important to be sensitive to the little embellishments that will occur, so that you can respond encouragingly while always being ready to return to the 'safe ground' of the usual pattern if the person seems to get anxious.

What is the point?

All of the people who are working to support a learner to explore the idea of communication and of being social should record details of, for example:

- what led up to a successful interaction?

- what intrigued or interested the learner?

- what common ground you discovered?

- how the learner showed their interest?

- how the learner responded to your responses?

- why you think the learner was interested?

- which of your responses seemed to maintain things or increase social interest?

- what the learner did to encourage you to continue?

- what was different from 'the usual'?

- how the learner/you terminated the 'game'?

Technique point

When you are actually 'in the moment' of an interaction, an important skill to develop is the ability to keep a watch for 'loops' that occur in what the person does, that is, sometimes the learner will return to something that got an interesting response from you 5 minutes ago. They might do so to test that 'it' still works; because nothing more interesting has happened since then; or simply because they liked what you did. While you might repeat your previous response, you might also slightly vary what you do ... even hesitating playfully before you answer with what seems to be your 'role' in an emerging game.

The record enables the people who work with the person to take advantage of each other's experiences: learning *what not to do* as much as *what to do*; what *types* of responses intrigue the learner; and which responses seemed to encourage the person you are supporting, to explore the situation. The more information you have as a practitioner, the more effectively you can support learning. Crucially, the spread of information across practitioners, ensures that those responding to the person's communicative or social explorations are more able to respond consistently and predictably when the person tries to strike up a 'conversation'.

Even if you are working alone, it is really useful to be able to prompt the memory to remember successful conversations or interesting 'topics' you have shared recently, so that you will be able to 'spot' them if they come up again.

It is vital that everyone who works with the person knows the story of how interactions have progressed and which topics seem to come up most frequently. The person learning about communication will learn best if she or he can see that their initiations are met with largely uniform responses. This does not mean that everyone should respond in exactly the same way, as that would end up being a bit wooden, and it is important that the person learns that different people have their own style of communication. However, the responses should be recognisable no matter who is responding – the major consideration is that responses should always be 'of' the person who is doing the learning.

Analogy

Communication is not a performance to be trained, it is an immensely complex process which defies task analysis or linear checklists. It is a process or activity which the learner explores through repeatedly exploring the boundaries of previous experiences, rather like gradually exploring or getting to know a new city. Taking this analogy further, the practitioner provides the security of a predictable structure of response, rather like a guide who, while not actually leading the learner anywhere, alerts them when they are passing something that might be interesting. The practitioner, as the 'guide' who is fluent with 'the map', can use their skills to suggest how to find the shops that they seem interested in, or offer routes for the learner to return to the places they enjoyed.

Medium term

As weeks and months pass by, you will begin to acquire a resource that describes the common themes, sequences and topics that your interactions tend to visit. If you have not already noticed that you seem to loop around the person's preferred topics – for example, exchanging blades of grass, tapping out rhythms, shaking beads, glancing and smiling, watching videos and sharing particular jingles, playing chase – a bi-monthly glance through your records will usually announce the patterns that have emerged.

The record will also describe the variety of ways you have responded (and the responses that your responses, in turn promoted), the best time or place to interact and the manner of response that the person or student clearly enjoys or is interested in. In addition, you will have a record of how simple exchanges have built into more prolonged dialogues, or how they have joined up or interconnected with others to form gently ritualised social games or established themes, or *formats*.

Long term

In any relationship, connections are made and bonds are built through finding areas of common ground. While initially conversations touch on aspects of shared interest and curiosity, as our friendship with someone develops, we usually revisit some topics of conversation we have had, to explore related lines of conversation. Additionally we periodically remind each other of the enjoyable experiences, events and moments of companionship that we have shared in the past. Just as relationships develop among friends around these conversations, emerging interactive partnerships with the people you are supporting also depend on building up repertoires of companionable activity which can be returned to.

As these repertoires emerge and become established, it is important not to let them become rigid or inflexible. As fluid, intuitive interactive partners, we can respond to the people we are supporting by doing something slightly different from our usual response to a situation, using, for example, hesitation or playful forgetfulness. While this interactive strategy keeps conversations spontaneous, it also sometimes provides a context for the learner to explore new possibilities.

Progress?

While with some people, you might identify the emergence or development of noticeable themes, with others you might not – you might simply have longer periods of attention, or a lesser degree of social withdrawal. The person might find it easier to maintain a constant state of arousal, or indeed not sleep as much as previously. Even after a year, you may have simply reached the point at which they joyfully recognise that something happened that they can distinguish as relating to a sound which they made. All of these represent progress. Progress is not necessarily vertical movement up a hierarchy of skill or finesse. For people with profound and complex intellectual disabilities, the notion of 'lateral progress' is equally valid – for example; the ability to share space with an increased range of other people; maintaining stable arousal with known people in different surroundings; maintaining social engagement for longer; or prolonged enjoyment of the difference between the sensations of responsive sounds or touches. The records that you make represent evidence of the person's *involvement*.

Using timelines

It is useful to reflect on how interactions have changed across prolonged periods so that progress and variation can be acknowledged and reported on, in the form of a record of achievement or involvement. It is important that we celebrate the contributions that the person you support has made in their journey and the record that is built up over a prolonged period of time (for example, a year) can be used to reflect on the periods when new strategies or interactive themes emerged, how they progressed and where they led to, on a timeline (see below).

- Jan 30 Luke immediately smiled (remembered from previous term?) when I imitated the sound he makes when he licked his lips.
- Feb 10 Luke turned his head slightly to try to look at me when I had been imitating his 'lip-smack' sound.
- Feb 15 Luke began to smile and lip-smack as soon as I sat next to him.
- March 15 Luke lip-smacked in a series of exchanges before getting tired.
- April 26 Luke approached me smiling and gazing – waited for me to lip smack.
- June 1 Luke approached me as usual and touched me when I hesitated before starting 'the game'.
- August 3 Luke gazed and vocalised when I 'stopped playing' half way through the game.
- Nov 25 Luke vocalised to get my attention then gazed, lip-smacked and waited for me to follow – I imitated vocal sound instead – he vocalised back to me, smiling.

Finally – the 'handover' record

Look at Figure 7.5 opposite. This is possibly one of the most important pieces of paperwork you can possibly create, as this record is used to inform:

- the next staff member to begin working with the person

- the staff member who will be working with them when you leave or are ill

- anybody else who might be involved in their life.

Although it was developed as a document which staff exchanged when a person made a transition between staff teams or services, it is also a document which describes what is happening *now* and should be routinely reviewed at least every six months. As you can see, the handover document contains information such as what anxiety looks like, where the person likes to be.

Describe what happens

It is assumed that the reader is familiar with the idea that when an interactive relationship is becoming established, it is always best to:

1. wait to see if the person approaches you, or

2. wait and watch for the sorts of activity the person enjoys, consider how you might respond encouragingly and communicatively; then wait for the person to return to the activity and gently approach them while trying to intrigue them by doing something similar to what they are doing.

Intensive Interaction information for_____ by_____

/   /20

Favourite place for interactions: e.g. classroom on floor/playground sitting on ground

What does she or he do to engage you? *If nothing…* how do **you** approach the learner for a 'game'?

E.g. *leads you to a special place [where?]* or *watches/tracks you* or *approaches you* or *offers you an object (what?)* or *vocalises and looks at you* or *touches you* or *gets close up to you*

DESCRIBE SOME OF THE DIFFERENT INTERACTIONS YOU SHARE
[NB do some games/formats/spirals come up regularly? What do they look like?]

What **doesn't** she or he like? (WHAT DO *DISTRESS/ANXIETY/DISPLEASURE* LOOK LIKE?)

(Continued)

(Continued)

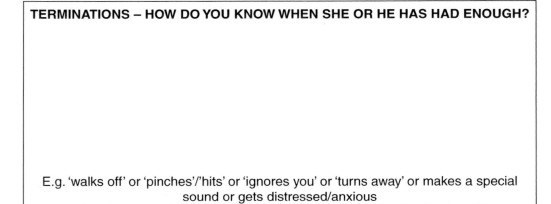

TYPE OF USUAL PHYSICAL CONTACT ROUTINELY, INVOLVED?
E.g. Which body areas? Does the student sit/lean on you or do you invite them to?
Is the physical contact central to the interactive sequence [e.g. exchanges
and physical dialogues], or comfort/presence focused?

DOES VIDEO EXIST OF THIS TYPE OF PHYSICAL CONTACT? Yes/No
HAVE PARENTS SEEN IT AT PSG? Yes/No

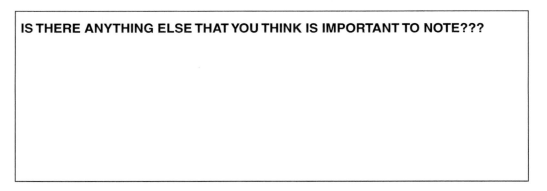

TERMINATIONS – HOW DO YOU KNOW WHEN SHE OR HE HAS HAD ENOUGH?

E.g. 'walks off' or 'pinches'/'hits' or 'ignores you' or 'turns away' or makes a special
sound or gets distressed/anxious

IS THERE ANYTHING ELSE THAT YOU THINK IS IMPORTANT TO NOTE???

Figure 7.5   The handover form

Photocopiable:
The Intensive Interaction Handbook © Dave Hewett, Graham Firth, Mark Barber and
Tandy Harrison, 2012 (Sage)

However, when the relationship is more established you might approach the person with the suggestion of a motif or game from one of the 'formats' or repertoires that you have built up together. On the handover document there is a place for you to describe these themes.

There is also a place to describe the type of physical contact that is typically used in interactions, this information might include strategies you use to avoid physical contact becoming too intimate or inappropriate, as well as strategies which you find useful to refocus the person's attempt to hug you (for example, standing side by side rather than standing face to face).

Recording using video

Video evidence is very useful, especially in schools or other formal settings where *evidence* of learning is appreciated as being important. Often, people with complex intellectual disabilities do not generate a trail of evidence that demonstrates the progress of their learning. Video can be very useful in fulfilling this requirement.

Video taken can be used as:

- evidence of involvement
- a record of learning
- a means of identifying progress.

It is also useful as:

- a resource for parents, carers and so on who are interested in learning how to respond in a manner which promotes interaction
- a point of reference to check whether something that you thought happened during an exchange, actually did happen
- a resource to help practitioners develop their Intensive Interaction skills – and to review whether you missed an opportunity or could have responded more clearly
- a resource to explain what Intensive Interaction is to your professional colleagues
- a record of achievement over an extended period.

Before looking at how video can be used:

- to encourage colleagues
- as evidence of learning
- as a means to identify progress
- as a record of achievement.

It will be valuable to consider some camera related issues.

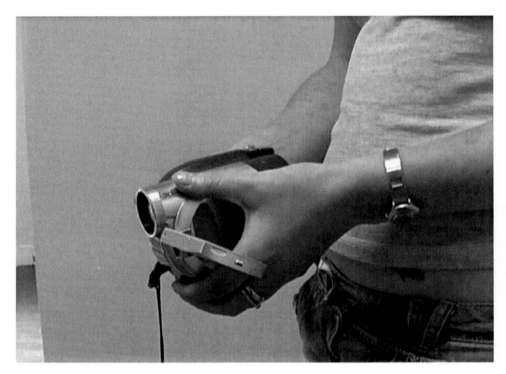

Holding the camera like this is relaxed and gives a steady shot

What sort of camera?

Video cameras can be the answer to many of your prayers or the beginning of a series of nightmares!!! It is important that they do not interfere with interaction. The idea is that they help!

A few simple rules for video cameras:

- The smaller and lighter they are, the harder they are to hold steady for more than a minute – even if they have image stabilisers.
  - Yes, you can consider using a tripod, but unless you have a clever 'claw' type of tripod, you will still have to hunt around for somewhere safe to put it … by which time the interaction has stalled.
  - Unless the interaction is very, very static, a tripod shoot probably will not be satisfactory.

- Big zoom ranges do not matter because the sound does not zoom in the same way as the lens does, so you get an image from far away, but you still get the sound of what is going on next to you.

- Most video cameras these days have a flip-open side door with a built-in viewer; when you try the camera before you buy it, check that you can see the image on this screen *when you are outdoors*. The cheaper the camera is, the less you will see.

- Buy a video camera that lets you film as long as possible before battery recharging is necessary.

- Cameras with built-in hard drives are best. Check with your shop that the camera automatically stores files as MPEGs.

Fill the frame with the people you are shooting

- Cameras with lots of fancy settings just intimidate your colleagues, even if you are a camera buff and you love to explain them.

    – The most important function is a good 'back-lit' function (that allows you to film while facing into light sources) although this will *still* not work if you are indoors, filming someone who is standing between the window and the camera.

Other considerations

- If the person you are filming is mobile, the camera needs to be too.

- The more you zoom to film a distant subject (that is, if you hold the camera to video an interaction on the other side of the room) the more 'camera-shake' you will get.

- A camera on a surface seems to attract other people in the room like a magnet – they will quickly come to know that picking up your camera will get your attention focused on them faster than almost anything else.

Using the camera: brief considerations

- When you are filming someone, hold the camera at about waist level and below the eye level of the people you are filming.

- Position yourself so that the learner's face is oriented to the camera.

- Do not zoom in too closely, but take care to fill the frame with the people involved.

- During interactions, keep the two people doing the interacting in the shot at all times.

- Do not zoom in and out once you have framed the action.

- Ensure that you are not pointing the camera into a strong light source (for example, a window). If you do, the camera will only record silhouettes.

FINALLY – KEEP FILMING AND *DON'T KEEP PRESSING 'PAUSE'.*

Practical issues

It is really important to have the camera charged at the start of the day/shift

Unless you are initiating the social game or an interaction that you know the person enjoys, or you have waited until you have seen something in their behaviour that you recognise as a potential 'jump off' point for a social interaction; we must assume that the learner might initiate a social dialogue with you … because they feel like it.

Do not assume that you will be approached at a time that is convenient for *your* schedule.

- Plan for flexibility.

BUT… I hear you say, or 'There are other really important things that we have to do in the day!' There simply is nothing that is more important than taking advantage of opportunities to help the person that you are supporting, to learn how to socialise and avoid isolation.

Put simply and starkly – for a human who has difficulty in this area, communication is the only important thing for them to learn. Without it there is no quality of life.

The truth is, that if you intend videoing an interaction with someone who can move around independently, then you need to have someone to do the filming for you; that is, someone who knows (ahead of time) how to use the camera

Some staff teams agree on an arrangement/rota that identifies the person who will film on that day, so that when an interaction 'gets airborne', someone can say 'would someone film for me'. This requires some planning. You might:

- decide to film at certain periods in the day

- decide to use the camera on a particular day of the week

- nominate a person to 'respond to the call' to film on a particular day – that is, that they will drop what they are currently involved in and come to you. That person might be a volunteer or it might be someone who just hates to see themselves on video. This requires extra effort, but it will be worth it. The camera person will be able to pick up again from where they left off. If you can only do this at certain times of the day, for example, when lots of staff are assembled in a day room or at recess time in a school, then that is your time. If you can use volunteers to do filming, use them … be pragmatic.

It is probably best, however, if the camera is always out of the bag, charged and ready to be picked up when an opportunity presents itself.

Does my bum look big?

Some people genuinely cannot cope with seeing themselves on video. Others simply get used to seeing themselves. You have two options if you want them to help:

1. Give them the video camera and encourage them to film you.

2. Give them time.

Storage

USB storage and 'flash drives' corrupt quickly, so always use a good *external hard drive*. Your camera will probably store your video as MPEG files automatically. Check before buying.

Saving files

- Your camera will allow you to 'drag and drop' files from its internal hard drive onto your external hard drive. After an hour of practice this will be second nature to you, even if you are not confident with ICT.

- Have a system for organising your files. Once you have several weeks worth of video, you will certainly come to regret *not* doing so.

- Organise files on your hard drive, with names – using, for example, YEAR > PERSON'S NAME > MONTH or DATE.

Using video evidence

This section describes how your video records of interaction can be used:

- as evidence of learning and progress

- as a record of achievement.

While parents may well be interested in this section, it is primarily focused on practitioners using Intensive Interaction in their workplace, that is, where professional development and evidence-based practices are central and formal considerations.

Using video as evidence of learning and progress

NB It is valuable to discuss your interest in Intensive Interaction with line managers in your organisation (for example, Assistant Principal, Unit/Shift Manager) and to confirm that individuals you might wish to video are not the subject of court orders, that is, within the remit of the organisation, there are no restrictions placed on generating an image of an individual for the purposes of individual records, plans, individual learning programmes (ILPs), IEPs, IPPs, person centred programmes (PCPs), and so on.

In addition to the written records you make of interactions, a video record might also usefully be made of every person you are working with at least once per fortnight. Apart from its use as a resource to help you to show others how the person likes to be approached, what sort of interaction they enjoy, how they show their involvement and where they like to be, as your video files build up you will get a record of the new and emerging 'formats' and dialogues that develop.

Try to find the best 10 minutes you have recorded over each two-week period.

To use video as evidence of progress or new learning, you will probably need to collate the videos you take over a number of months. This clearly takes some organisation and equipment to store your footage. Be organised and always include the date in the file name when you save it to your hard drive as things get very complicated very quickly as your library of video increases.

When the time comes to write reports or review progress, look at video from when you started recording it and compare it to video of more recent interactions.

NB Always keep your first ever piece of video as the starting point.

When you compare the two pieces of interaction, look for differences, for elaboration. Progress is not necessarily a 'finished' skill – it might be seen in the way that an interaction takes a different path from the usual one, or that the person does something which you have noticed them doing when they were involved in a different topic, or in the way the person watches you to see what you are going to do ... shows signs of anticipation ... or when you hesitate, they 'suggest' or lead you to the action they thought you should make. Progress is usually seen in terms of the increase in the diversity of what have previously been quite predictable sequences or routes that games take.

Use the fundamentals of communication (Nind and Hewett, 2001), as reference points for differences in:

- increased enjoyment of being with another person

- the ability to attend to that person

- the ability to concentrate and length of attention span

- using more elaborate sequences of activity with another person

- the ability to take turns in exchanges of behaviour

- the ability to share personal space

- using and understanding eye contacts

- using and understanding facial expressions

- using and understanding physical contacts

- using and understanding other non-verbal communications

- vocalising and using vocalisations meaningfully (including speech)

- the ability to regulate and control arousal levels.

Or simply look for evidence of, for example:

- new responses, initiations and directing behaviours

- increasing range of facial expressions

- emerging vocalisations

- body responses approaching gestures

- more effective use of gaze to effect changes in the communication exchange

- greater tolerance

- spontaneous participation

- increased observation of others

- waiting for a turn

- decrease in withdrawal from others

- engaging others in physical dialogues

- new variations

- awareness of cause and effect

- looking for expected response

- visually tracking a familiar adult in anticipation of a game (M. Kellett and M. Nind, 2003).

Remember that while the interactive activities or formats that you return to, might seem very 'samey' to you, the person who is doing the learning is often using this predictable structure as a context within which they can explore where the boundaries of predictability end and a new 'topic' or result begins. These spirals of activity can be the familiar background noise that helps them to feel secure, or the reliable jump off point that they can return to if an interaction becomes too unfamiliar.

Framework for recognising progress

NB *If you work in schools, these levels might be known to you as the 'P' levels.*

Because the learner's progress can be very tangibly tied in with the development in the variety and diversity of a range of interactive activities, you might decide to use a more formal or developmental way of recording progress. Many teams or 'communities of practice' use a framework of statements that describe a spectrum of progress to 'judge' or 'moderate' progress.

Look at a 10-minute piece of video you have. Then look at the statements below. Find the statement which describes what you see in the video. Do not pay too much attention to *the name of the level*, focus on the sentences in the statement – they are very carefully worded.

Encounter

The person is present during an experience or activity without any obvious learning outcome, although for some people, for example those who withhold their attention or their presence from many situations, their willingness to tolerate a shared activity may, in itself, be significant.

Awareness

The person appears to show awareness that something has happened and notice, fleetingly focus on or attend to an object, event or other person, for example, by briefly interrupting a pattern of self-absorbed movement or vocalisation.

Attention and response

The person attends and begins to respond, often not consistently, to what is happening, for example, by showing signs of surprise, enjoyment, frustration or dissatisfaction, demonstrating the beginning of an ability to distinguish between different people, objects, events and places.

Engagement

The person shows more consistent attention to, and can tell the difference between, specific events in their surroundings, for example, by focused looking or listening; turning to locate objects, events or people; following moving objects and events through movements of their eyes, head or other body parts.

Participation

The person engages in sharing, taking turns and the anticipation of familiar sequences of events, for example, by smiling, vocalising or showing other signs of excitement, although these responses may be supported by staff or other pupils.

Involvement

The person actively strives to reach out, join in or comment in some way on the activity itself or on the actions or responses of the other people, for example, by making exploratory hand and arm movements, seeking eye contact with staff or other pupils, or by speaking, signing or gesturing.

Using video evidence to encourage colleagues

NB It is assumed that at the time of reading this, the reader has already discussed their interest in Intensive Interaction with the colleagues they are working with. It is also assumed that the reader has captured some footage of an interaction.

Video is a powerful tool and you can use it to illustrate what you are trying to achieve and how the person responds to you when you do Intensive Interaction, to the people you work with.

Once you have 10-minutes of video, it is time to be *daring*.

Phase 1

- Put some articles/books/a DVD/miscellaneous resources in the staffroom.

- Put some photographs of you and the person you are working with involved in Intensive Interaction, somewhere prominent, for example, a corridor display.

Phase 2

- Talk to your manager and ask if you can show your video to your colleagues at a staff meeting.

- Look carefully at the video and try to pre-empt any questions you might be asked – get a sympathetic colleague to look at it before the staff meeting and note their questions.

Phase 3

- After the staff meeting, advertise a further meeting for people who were interested, to discuss and reflect on what you know.

    NB at your mini-meetings always have

    - *chocolate biscuits*

    - *non-elastic end-of-meeting time*

    - *agenda (with an invitation to next meeting, to your manager as it is crucial to have her or his continued support).*

Phase 4

Set up a regular time to meet as a:

- 'core group'

- 'special interest group'

- 'Intensive Interaction group'

- video, coffee and cake group.

Meanwhile you should be demonstrating good Intensive Interaction practice:

- at recess

- in corridors

- in public areas, that is, *as well as in the room where you spend most of your time.*

Phase 5

As your meetings become regular you might hit a slump in 'what to do'. You should consider the following ideas as topics of conversations with your colleagues:

- *Start-stop video*

    – Play your video again and press pause every 2 minutes, asking the questions (see 'start-stop video' box).

Activity: start-stop video

1. Play 2 minutes of your 10-minute video.
2. Question to colleagues – What is the topic of the conversation?
3. Question to colleagues – What is the person focusing on?
4. Question to colleagues – What do you think I am focusing on?
5. Question to colleagues – What else might the person do – that is, what other motifs of activity have you noticed them do when you have watched them previously and how might I respond if they start *them?*
6. What might happen next?
7. PRESS PLAY AGAIN AND WATCH FOR 2 MORE MINUTES then REPEAT.

- *Victories and defeats*

    – Compare your good news, wow moments, problems.

- *Show and tell*

    – Does anyone else have video?

- *Moderation*

    – Get your colleagues to find a statement from the 'framework' that they think best describes what happens on your video, and if it is different from the statement you chose, have an open discussion where everyone explains their thinking – look for dialogue not a debate (see debate versus dialogue below).

- *Recording*

    – If you have five people in a room watching the same video, ask them to write down what happened and compare notes on what you all thought was important – it is great practice and makes for interesting discussion (and reflective practice).

- *Discuss articles*

    – Print off some articles from one of the websites and have a sort of 'book club' discussion about what you each got from it.

- *Network*

    – Use the Intensive Interaction Networks, contact other people working and living nearby to meet with.

Debate is oppositional: two opposing sides try to prove each other wrong. Dialogue is collaborative: individuals with differing perceptions work towards shared understanding.

Debate is oppositional: two opposing sides try to prove each other wrong. In dialogue one listens to understand, to make meaning, and to find common ground.

> In debate one listens to find flaws, to spot differences and to counter arguments. Dialogue enlarges and possibly changes a participant's point of view: debate defends assumptions as truths.
>
> Debate creates a closed minded attitude: a determination to be right. Dialogue creates an open-minded attitude: an openness to being wrong and an openness to change.
>
> In debate one submits one's best thinking and defends it against challenge to show that it is right. In dialogue one submits one's best thinking, expecting that other people's reflections will help improve it rather than threaten it.
>
> (Acknowledging J. Williamson, personal communication, 1996)

We have moved across a broad range of issues around maintaining and continuing the process of Intensive Interaction. While you may be the only person using Intensive Interaction at present, it is still very useful to record what you are doing, how the person you are supporting to communicate is responding to you and what sorts of activities you explore with them.

If you are doing Intensive Interaction at work and making a record to enable your service to better address the needs of the person, do not be distracted or intimidated by dire warnings of data protection – your record is simply that, a record of what you are doing and how a person is learning.

 Four things to bear in mind when you call a meeting

1. NEVER finish later than you promised – people have lives to lead and people to pick up after work; do not make them late.
2. ALWAYS provide goodies (for example, chocolate biscuits and some fruit).
3. ALWAYS have a scribe who takes minutes for the group and keeps a file copy.
4. Send a copy to your department manager. Experience says that they are the key to the success of your group. You are contributing to professional discussion and to the positive development of your service – do not be bashful.

Gaining a person's consent to film them may be held up as an issue, and you should check your workplace practices and policies. Given the purposes for which you are using the records, you might consider requesting the consent of the person's family or advocate.

The video record is for professional use and not to be used or displayed outside of the context of supporting the person to learn. *Clearly you will not be posting it on the Internet.* Check to see if you should store it on-site, or in a secure space/file.

Remember: Do not store it outside of the context you use it for.

Unless you are using it for purposes outside the service you work in, your record is quite innocuous. If you are using video, the *method* of keeping a record may be novel, but essentially, it is the same as the records that are kept usually.

Good luck

I hope this chapter has given you a wealth of ideas to help you to begin making a record of the sorts of interactions that a person enjoys and the way that they demonstrate their enjoyment. There have also been suggestions and ideas for practitioners who wish to chart the changes and increasing complexities that occur during interactions, as well as strategies for encouraging the involvement of colleagues.

All the documents are there for you to use, but they are all 'work in progress', that is, they are constantly being changed and refined – you should adapt them to fit your needs and the requirements of your particular setting.

Intensive Interaction always works best if done within a 'community of practice'. It is very difficult to sustain if you are a lone practitioner. You do not have to be an 'expert' to bring colleagues together into a forum, and you should not feel the need to be able to supply all of the answers.

Good luck!

References

Kellett, M. and Nind, M. (2003) *Implementing Intensive Interaction in Schools: Guidelines for Practitioners, Managers and Coordinators.* London: David Fulton.

Nind, M. and Hewett, D. (2001) *A Practical Guide to Intensive Interaction.* Kidderminster: BILD.

8

Supporting Intensive Interaction in workplaces

Graham Firth and Dave Hewett

This chapter looks at:

- **The environment**
- **Best working atmosphere for supporting Intensive Interaction work?**
- **Methodical, organised collaboration**
- **Settings: special schools**
     Integrating Intensive Interaction with other work and approaches
- **Settings: adult residential and day services**
- **Settings: the Interactive Café.**

In this chapter we offer some general advice on workplace issues for supporting Intensive Interaction practice. We will try to provide a vision of the 'best-case' scenario in most respects, while also attempting not be overly prescriptive. Successful workplaces take many forms. Our apologies – we may at times be offering some advice that feels obvious to some readers.

The environment

The environment in which we attempt to develop Intensive Interaction with our clients or pupils can be a very important factor in getting it right. It is often useful to think about the environment even before we start. We might need to arrange for certain things to be present, for example, a comfortable place to sit together, a settee or adjacent beanbags, or a thick woolly rug on the floor. We might also need to arrange for certain other things to be absent, for example, a distracting television in the room, or an unsupportive fellow staff member.

It might also be useful to do some initial observations so that we can think about the person themselves and their preferences:

- Do they have a favourite room, or a place they seem most relaxed? What are its features? What is there, and what is not?

- Do they usually sit in the same chair, or the same place within a room? Why might that be?

- Do they seem more approachable at certain times, in certain places? What is going on? Who is around? What are they doing?

If we spend some time trying to answer these questions, then this reflective process might make us consider more aspects of the environment than we might have done at first glance – and we can then act in the light of any thoughts that occur, and thus we are more likely to make the environment more Intensive Interaction friendly in that way.

If the person you are working with or supporting spends most of their time in a wheel-chair, then it will be worthwhile thinking about how you position yourself (both comfortably and safely – remember bad backs can result from poor positioning!) and about where the person is themselves – have they chosen this place for themselves?

Might there be a better place to interact, where the noise levels and lighting, and the warmth (or lack of it), and the amount of distraction or general hustle and bustle (or lack of it) might be more conducive to Intensive Interaction? Where would that place be? Is it already available or will you have to arrange for it to be available?

To create the ideal environment there might be some physical aspects that need to be planned for:

- Can you arrange any chairs in a more Intensive Interaction friendly way, that is, should the chairs be side by side, or directly face to face, or at a certain angle (often when chairs are placed at about a 90° angle this can make Intensive Interaction more relaxed and easy – you do not end up too directly in someone's face, but eye contact and sharing of personal space in this position can often seem less demanding of the person)?

- Do you need to put out mats or beanbags, or might you need a hoist?

- Are there any sensory resource items available that the person likes to explore and can be used in joint-focus activities?

It might also be useful to think about any visual or hearing impairments that a person may have, as these factors will be important in creating the ideal environment in which to engage the person – it might be necessary to create a quieter environment or to adjust the lighting (or your positioning with respect to the available light – e.g. with a window behind you) to maximise the potential for successful interactivity.

Possibly the most important aspect, and sometimes the least controllable aspect of creating an ideal Intensive Interaction environment, is the presence of other people. It might be useful to ask yourself whether the other people in the room will have a positive and encouraging effect on any Intensive Interaction, or whether they might have the opposite effect, that is, their presence will potentially have a negative and distracting effect (such people might include other students, residents or clients, or they might be fellow staff members). If this is the case, can you do something about it?

Finally, you might need to think about any environmental 'safety' issues that might need addressing – these issues might include any trip hazards for ambulant people (objects on the floor, furniture too near doorways, exposed electrical leads, and so on), or choking hazards for people who might explore smaller items with their mouths, or cleanliness issues such as access to hand-washing facilities if someone drools saliva or has manual exploration issues in certain private places! During actual Intensive Interaction sessions the availability of alcohol gel or wet-wipes might suffice.

So, generally you should be looking at all the environmental factors that might influence the potential success of any Intensive Interaction work that you plan to do. You should always be looking to maximise the positive and supportive environmental aspects (for example, intelligent positioning of furniture, availability of supportive people, good levels of warmth and light, and so on) and you should also always be looking to minimise the potentially negative and distracting environmental aspects (television, distracting people, potential safety issues, and so on).

Best working atmosphere for supporting Intensive Interactive work?

One word springs to mind immediately for a description of the most Intensive Interaction supporting atmosphere – *relaxed*. There can be confusions about this word – many people can interpret it as something like: 'well, we're all gonna be kind of slow you know, and laid back, things get done when they get done, it doesn't matter too much if they don't get done as long as we have a good Karma, you know ...'

Perhaps there is a better phrase in order to assist those of us who see being relaxed as an excuse for indolence or those managers or practitioners who see being 'relaxed' as a negative state of being where things don't get done properly. Let us say, rather, *'relaxed purposefulness'*. Everything is going to get done. Everything is going to be planned and methodical. However, we will proceed in a relaxed fashion in a relaxed atmosphere while being highly purposeful.

This is not a small matter, being relaxed and proceeding in a relaxed fashion is literally at the core of the Intensive Interaction technique. It is also at the centre of the state of being there for the other person. People who are at early stages of development need to be feeling relaxed too, as well as comfortable, safe, secure, confident, supported. If they do not feel these things they probably will not learn.

In previous chapters we have described the enemies of Intensive Interaction practice:

- haste

- stress

- unhappiness.

Intensive Interaction practitioners need to be:

- unhurried

- relaxed

- available

- purposeful

- methodical/organised

- collaborative.

Which of those two lists applies more in your workplace? We cannot give you too much guidance in this chapter on how to achieve a shift from the first list to the second if that is what is needed. There are whole books written about that topic. However, perhaps a start would be to make sure the whole team reads this chapter (actually this book).

Methodical, organised collaboration

In our fantasy best-case scenario team, the members of the team collaborate effectively. First, they are good communicators with each other. It is virtually certain that this will be a positive force in the communication work with the pupils or service users. They talk in detail about the work with each person, they share with delight the bits and pieces of progress each day, they discuss with each other about how each of *them* are feeling. This team also collaborates effectively with professionals who are not part of the team – crucially, for instance, the speech and language therapist.

This team has systems organised so the service user or pupil is at the centre of everything, and then the routines of the staff are organised around that in order to keep the other person at the centre. Many workplaces do it the other way around.

An Intensive Interaction supporting workplace will have communication as the absolute first priority in everything that takes place. Again, this seems obviously necessary, yet it is not always the case. Many establishments for people with severe learning difficulties (SLD) do not operate with communication work as the priority.

This priority will show itself in the way the activities and learning sessions are organised. More working time will be devoted to communication than any other activity. As has been detailed in previous chapters, Intensive Interaction time needs to be available in an organised fashion, but also in such a way that there can be spontaneity and a sense of seizing the moment. If the day and the timetable are too tightly regulated, the way of organising could be counterproductive.

There will also be an embracing of the philosophy of 'interactivity' – the Intensive Interaction, or indeed all communication work, running as a thread or theme throughout everything that takes place. Members of staff recognise the need to change the emphasis of an activity with spontaneity from, say, learning how to make a cup of tea, to simply engaging in a pleasurable communication exchange. Or, indeed, making sure that any activity is also such a communication activity.

Even a relaxed team is a team that plans well and methodically. Actually, good planning is essential in order to feel relaxed and confident. Those times when you absolutely do not need to be in a hurry need to be planned and scheduled. In order to achieve this, it may be necessary not to plan in too much. There can be a temptation to try to pack too much into the day as a demonstration of how hard we are all working.

So, overall, there should be no sense of 'laissez-faire'. This relaxed, purposeful team has scheduled itself to be like that.

This team also takes a pride and a pleasure in the record-keeping. In this book we offer advice on recording, but also stress that it should be enjoyable – the pay-off for all your efforts. Teams working in a good atmosphere realise this and share the enterprise of keeping track of people's progress as a pleasurable routine.

Settings: special schools

How about this as a statement of overall attitude or ethos?

> A school for children who have severe learning difficulties is a school that is there to work on communication. It works on the teaching of some other things as well.

We recommend this as a starting point for a successful and effective SLD school. How many children in such a school – including the ones who we term as being of 'higher ability' – have actually completed communication learning?

In the classroom:

- Plan for plenty of time on communication work every day as the first priority in planning the timetable.

- Discuss the nature of the concept of 'interactivity' and work together to have it running as a thread through all other activities.

- Recognise and discuss the reality of where the pupils are developmentally 'at' and plan accordingly to make sure that for instance, they receive plenty of general 'early learning'-type activities.

- This may mean 'opening up' the day a little and including provision of sessions that are more like play sessions in early years (read the Early Years Foundation Stage guidance for some assistance).

- Such sessions provide maximum opportunity for one-to-one time with members of staff rotating among the pupils opportunistically.

- Discuss, plan and practise for care support, for instance in the bathroom, also being one-to-one communication time.

- Use visual displays to emphasise communication issues and the communication 'atmosphere'.

- Every day make a communication note in the home–school book.

- Do everything possible to ensure that all communication work is transferred to and shared with the parents.

- Make sure that each child has a communication passport giving detailed information on their communication abilities and the routines of how to interact with each of them.

- Consider doing the communication passport in a PowerPoint file on a CD-ROM, this would enable video clips to be included.

- Collaborate in all respects with the speech and language therapist – use her or him, for instance, for more independent observations of pupil progress.

General school issues:

- Ideally, the school will have a communication curriculum document or other such written guidance, that emphasises the priority nature of communication work and gives detail about practices and techniques.

- Ideally, the communication curriculum will be a bigger document than any other on teaching and learning.

- The document will describe and support the sorts of classroom initiatives discussed in the previous section.

- It seems an obviously good idea to have a senior post with specified responsibility for communication work within the curriculum.

- While being written for pupils in early years, the Early Years Foundation Stage guidance is very useful as a resource for thinking about all areas of early learning.

- Communication work should feature regularly on the schedule of in-service training (INSET) or other training.

- Most schools already know that the speech and language therapist is a powerful and precious resource. Use this person.

Integrating Intensive Interaction with other work and approaches

Intensive Interaction is a gentle approach to teaching and learning that is based on scientific understandings as to how human beings learn. Therefore, it does have a certain heritage from the psychological research on which it is based. All the approaches that are in use in our work are likely to have one heritage or another. For instance, many of the working approaches and techniques that are used in schools have their origin in the work of behavioural psychologists such as B.F. Skinner.

Intensive Interaction, as previously described, has its origins in the work of cognitive or developmental psychologists such as Jerome Bruner, Daniel Stern and Rudolph Schaffer (see Chapter 3). Many of our approaches are different from one another in their origins and the way in which they operate. However:

- In the first place, Intensive Interaction should not conflict with anything else that you do. It is a gentle, almost inoffensive way of working that will not damage anything else.

- It can coexist with, for instance picture exchange communication system (PECS) or other behavioural approaches, without making immediate, obvious problems.

- Yet, you may gradually feel that some other approaches may conflict with Intensive Interaction. For instance, in a general, organisational sense, some approaches may ask you to be quite 'programmed' and driven through the day. For certain periods of the day you will then change tempo and atmosphere for doing Intensive Interaction. Perhaps this is not a problem; perhaps it does not feel right to make this switch.

Over the long term:

- Doing Intensive Interaction may cause a rethink of much of what you do as the power of 'interactivity' becomes apparent and the pupil or service user makes progress.

- You may start to re-evaluate other approaches you use and the way that the pupil or service user is addressed by the working practices.

- Doing Intensive Interaction may further cause a team to rethink on concepts of 'personhood' and what are the ultimate aims of your work in terms of outcomes for the person.

Settings: adult residential and day services

Adult residential and day services, or support services more generally, often have many advantages when they work using Intensive Interaction. Regular contact with a service user, and contact in places whose physical and social environment can be deliberately adapted to support Intensive Interaction working, should make Intensive Interaction relatively easy to implement, especially if done with a stable, well-trained, well-supported and well-supervised staff team.

In fact, we will often say that although Intensive Interaction was developed as a teaching approach within classrooms, its relaxed and free-flowing nature fits perhaps better with the (hopefully) relaxed nature of the person's home and the support the staff provide there. Much of the early take-up and support for Intensive Interaction in the late 1980s came from adult services. It seemed that these services were much more open and flexible at that time than special education was able to be.

 Adult day services have been moving towards providing more sessional services, with services less centred on a particular service building. More time is now being spent on supporting service users to access community activity, and this is certainly a welcome change for many day service users. However there are some, actually a significant number of service users, who will gain very little from nominal community participation or a raised community profile. Indeed, for many service users with more severe or profound learning difficulties Intensive Interaction should be seen as a mainstay of their daily activity. We should never be afraid to point this out!

However, in reality some services have to work in far from ideal circumstances, both in terms of their physical environments and the levels of appropriately trained and supervised staff. At times the working cultures of some services can be more focused on appearing to fill a service user's time (with a range of recognisable 'activities') rather than identifying and then appropriately responding to a person's particular communicative strengths and social preferences.

The introduction of Intensive Interaction in any service should be planned with longer-term sustainability and service development in mind. Intensive Interaction induction and training should be an ongoing process and involve all the staff, so that even those staff members who do not become directly involved with using Intensive Interaction will at least understand what is going on, and what outcomes are expected (one outcome being that they will eventually be required to join in!).

 ### Speech and language therapists

Do you have support from speech and language therapy services? If not, try and get some. Speech and language therapists have been some of the most powerful people in the dissemination of Intensive Interaction. They are a knowledgeable, essential support.

Once again we advise the power of documentation. There is an increasing focus on the writing of policies and guidelines, mostly for good reasons, though we can feel a bit swamped. However, as you facilitate and establish Intensive Interaction practice, make sure that you discuss with the team the production of guidelines and explanatory documents on this area of work. Do not let Intensive Interaction be something left on the side, not part of the 'proper' work.

Settings: the Interactive Café

An 'Interactive Café' is a pre-planned and yet informal social occasion that is specifically set up to support the use of Intensive Interaction with identified service users or clients. The relaxed café atmosphere is created to make everyone feel welcome, no matter how difficult they generally find social interactivity or how profound their intellectual disability.

The basic idea behind the Interactive Café was to disseminate the general message of Intensive Interaction, and at the same time, to increase the opportunities for everyone who might benefit from the approach to engage in and enjoy Intensive Interactions.

During each 'Interactive Café' session experienced Intensive Interaction practitioners are present to facilitate the occasion. These practitioners are available to use Intensive Interaction directly with any visiting service users. These facilitators can also offer advice on implementing Intensive Interaction to any support staff or carers who attend, and answer any other questions concerning the use of the approach.

In this way, the support staff present can see directly what Intensive Interaction might look like with the person they support. This enables the support staff or carers to realise that the skills necessary to 'do' Intensive Interaction are not 'out of the ordinary' in any way, and that Intensive Interaction is almost certainly well within their current capabilities.

During the 'Interactive Café' sessions:

- appropriate 'easy to read' Intensive Interaction literature and hand-outs are available

- Intensive Interaction DVD footage might also be shown on any available television or laptop

- Intensive Interaction training application forms can also be left out for anyone that might be interested

- other items made available might include various sensory or resource items that might be useful in creating and supporting joint focus interactions with specific service users

- drinks and biscuits are usually made available at some point as well.

As people visit more regularly, everyone gets to know each other, and the café can provide a comfortable arena for staff to share their experiences, and possibly their concerns, about the approach with other staff and their service users.

 The 'Interactive Café' was originally facilitated in Leeds by Graham Firth and specialist speech and language therapist Marion Crabbe – the first session being at Potternewton Fulfilling Lives Service in early 2006. Since then, in Leeds, café sessions have been held in a large number of different service locations (mainly in a series of six to eight weekly sessions), and it still continues to provide inclusive and genuinely sociable occasions for those people who are supported to attend.

Further reading 📖

Kellett, M. and Nind, M. (2003) *Implementing Intensive Interaction in Schools: Guidance for Practitioners, Managers and Coordinators*. London: David Fulton.

Skinner, B.F. (1938) *The Behavior of Organisms*. New York: Appleton-Century-Crofts.

B.F. Skinner is known for his experiments on learning with rats and pigeons. His type of technique is often referred to as 'operant conditioning'.

For a further technical review of some of these issues, see for instance: Hewett, D. (2011) 'What is Intensive Interaction? Curriculum, process and approach', in D. Hewett (ed.), *Intensive Interaction: Theoretical Perspectives*. London: Sage.

9

Doing Intensive Interaction at home

Tandy Harrison

This chapter looks at:

- **Learning how to make connections**
- **Finding the moments and places**
- **Sometimes he is under the weather**
- **Other family members and friends**
- **Relating to the professionals**
- **Record-keeping in the family**
- **Parents in a 'community of practice'.**

When they are expecting a child, most people anticipate doing lovely things with that child in the future, maybe chatting around a dinner table, baking cakes together, setting up a train set. The possibilities seem endless. If you have a child with a learning disability, things can turn out very differently from how you had imagined. You may be faced with a situation where your child lacks the motivation and the skills to interact with you, even in simple ways. For parents this can be very distressing and isolating. You find yourself going through the moves of caring for your child, but having no real sense of a meaningful bond with them. If they do not play or respond like typical children, how do we as parents begin to shape things between us?

Learning how to make connections

On top of this, we parents are often faced with conflicting advice and well-meaning different types of therapy, which may be helpful but which often do not address our central concern, namely, how to have some sort of relationship with our child. More than anything we want to know how to have some moments where we have a sense of connection with our child, and have fun together.

One of the dangers is, that in our eagerness to establish rapport with our child, we are not relaxed enough when we set time aside for Intensive Interaction. We want results

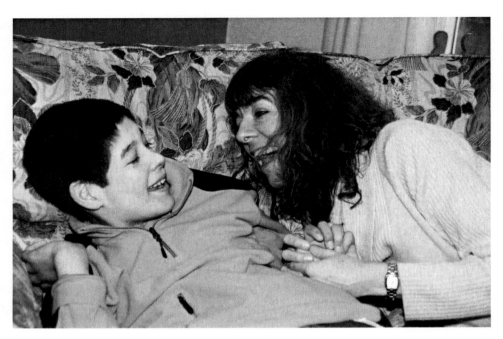

Sharing a joke without words

and we judge ourselves if we do not get them. This can end up with us intending to try Intensive Interaction with a lot of thoughts other than being present, relaxed, unhurried and flexible, which are essential for the approach to flow and be enjoyable.

The tips in Chapter 4, on mental preparation, are therefore really helpful and worth reading through again before you begin. I found that when I started to use the approach with George, if I set time aside formally to do Intensive Interaction, I was less relaxed and it did not really happen. I found it more useful to try the approach at times which occurred naturally in the rhythm of the day when I was already with my son, such as at the end of afternoon snack time in the kitchen, on the trampoline or at bath time.

As I got more used to doing Intensive Interaction, I found that I was using it just as a way of being with him, around the house. Sometimes for a few moments while getting breakfast ready, sometimes after school in the sitting room or on our bed for much longer periods. The important thing is to try it out without pressurising yourself. Just spending time with your child, being present with them and following their lead feels good, and helps you to feel closer to them, even if in the early stages you get little back. You begin to notice small changes as you 'hang out' with them and very gradually get to know them. As you get used to the approach, you naturally find that more opportunities for using it arise.

Finding the moments and places

If you would like to explore Intensive Interaction with your child, but are unsure how to start, see if you can identify times of day in your family routine when things are not too frenetic and when you are with your child anyway. For families with a child under school age, this is usually much easier than for those with older children.

It gets trickier to find 'one-to-one' slots around the school day, particularly if you are juggling the needs of other children in your family too. At the beginning, when you are trying the approach out for yourself, try to find windows of time when other children have gone off to do homework or play independently. Five minutes is enough to give it a go. The open-ended nature of Intensive Interaction means that you can fit it in around existing family routines.

We can also view those times when we attend to our child's personal needs, like nappy or pad changing times and baths, as natural opportunities to use Intensive Interaction. Bath time has always been one of the times my son and I have our most varied interactions. Sometimes we have long 'conversations' made up of a mixture of vocal noises, body movements, splashes, water pouring and knocking or banging the side of the bath. Now he gives lots of eye contact, and smiles and laughs while we are playing. It is during times like these that I have a profound sense that his relationship with me, as his Mum, is distinct and special. In fact I have noticed that as different adults in his life use Intensive Interaction as a way to interact with him, over time he has developed different interactive routines or games with each of them. It has been a way for him to develop real friendships, all different from each other, in the same way that my friendships vary in nature.

Weekends and holidays may afford many more varied opportunities to be together so you can try out the approach in different places, both indoors and out, at home and elsewhere. You may be a parent of a child who has grown up and is living independently, in which case you could use Intensive Interaction when you have opportunities to visit them and when they come home.

As parents engaging in Intensive Interaction with our children at home, the types of interaction we will experience will vary hugely, depending on the age, personalities and abilities of our children, as well as our individual circumstances. Some parents may find their child needs a quiet, undisturbed place to engage. If you are the parent of someone with profound and multiple learning disabilities, you may find that you spend time quietly with your child, tuning in and responding to very subtle movements, like blinking, breathing or slight head movements. Alternatively, your child might be very active physically, and you may find yourself doing a fair bit of bouncing on a bed or 'rough and tumble' physical interactions. The varied examples of Intensive Interaction scenarios in schools and residential settings given in Chapter 5 would apply equally to those of us at home.

It is helpful to approach Intensive Interaction with a spirit of curiosity, so do not be afraid to experiment by trying it out in different places at home and at different times of day, to see what works best for your child and for you. As a parent, you will know the times of day to avoid, when your child needs some 'down time' or is tired. If your child's mobility is restricted, you might like to try Intensive Interaction when they are in different positions; either in their wheelchair or on the floor with suitable support. Gradually you will find that you will build up a repertoire of interactions that may vary from place to place, which you can repeat and expand on. Some may be very short and others much longer. Remember to read your child's signs for when they have had enough and never 'push' them to keep playing, however much you might be enjoying it! At the moment I end up doing lots of short interactions based on vocal and movement imitation in the kitchen, longer interactions based on songs or rolling a ball in the living room, and jumping, singing, tickling and squeezing games on our bed, and on the trampoline outside.

Sometimes he is under the weather

When you have got Intensive Interaction going with your child, and know what sort of interactive routines or games they like, you may find they have odd days or short phases where they do respond, but are less responsive and less interactive than usual. This is usually linked to being a bit under the weather, maybe after an illness, or tiredness. There are days with my son when I do not know what the reason is, but then we all have days when we feel less inclined to be social. At these times your interactions are likely to be quieter, simpler and perhaps have a less connected feel than usual. Sometimes I end up lying next to George, my son, on days like this, having a very slow and quiet exchange of hand stroking or finger touching. It feels quite different to what I think of as our usual sort of interactions. When you are the interactive partner to the same person over a long period of time, you find that the nature of interactions will vary according to their moods, health, where you are, the changing pattern of their interests, even the time of year. In summer you might be using your garden or an outdoor area much more, for instance.

Other family members and friends

I have mentioned finding a time to be on your own with your child when you are starting off, getting used to the feel of doing Intensive Interaction yourself. Once you are getting the hang of it, you will naturally start to use it more in all sorts of everyday situations, which will involve you and your child interacting in this way around other people. It is a really good idea to explain why you are doing it to those around you, particularly spouses, partners, other children and other close family members like grandparents. The most important thing, I find, is to feel understood and supported by other people when using Intensive Interaction. Not all of them may feel comfortable taking on the approach themselves, but that does not matter if their attitude is supportive of those in the family who are actually doing it. We all know the old saying 'actions speak louder than words'. Very often people who see Intensive Interaction in action, who watch the unfolding responses between those doing it, and the 'bubble' of connection that can result, will understand why you are doing it.

If other family members are keen to use Intensive Interaction too, so much the better! There have been moving moments in my professional life, as a family support worker, when I've watched siblings really click with their brother or sister with a learning difficulty, using Intensive Interaction. To an outsider it might have looked like somewhat unusual play, but that is unimportant when the fun and togetherness are there. The benefits of other people at home using the approach will be more interactions and social opportunities for your child and closer relationships with a range of people. You could say that they are going to be more fully included in family life, from a relationships perspective. Those using Intensive Interaction with the child will be able to share experiences and perceptions, as well as support each other in using the approach.

You might find yourself using Intensive Interaction around strangers too, as you explore different environments to try it out in. I have found that swimming pools are places where my son is really switched on to Intensive Interaction. I also find myself doing imitative vocal and movement games and interactive singing games as we wait for food in restaurants, at checkouts or in waiting rooms. You get the odd funny look, but most people are fine with it. As always, use Intensive Interaction when you are feeling relaxed, and always read your child's response.

It is almost inevitable that parents who like using Intensive Interaction become advocates for it, because we end up explaining to other people what we are doing so often. This can be really tiring at times, on top of the rest of our lives, looking after a disabled child, the rest of our family, our work, and so on. We also know we will be providing significant care for our children in different ways for many years. It is important for us to be aware of our own needs and give ourselves time for the things that we find replenishing, so that we can maintain our energy levels.

Relating to the professionals

If your child is benefiting from Intensive Interaction it would be good to share what you are doing at home with professionals you are involved with, as well as school, college, respite or residential staff, as appropriate. If the approach is helping your child make progress and providing them with more inclusive experiences, then it is important that they get as much of it as possible and that those involved work together.

Maybe some of the professionals you are in contact with are experienced Intensive Interaction practitioners already. If you are not sure, you could begin by finding out whether the individuals supporting you have any experience of Intensive Interaction, whether they have had any formal training, and whether their organisation uses Intensive Interaction. You could ask for copies of communication policies to see if Intensive Interaction is mentioned.

If Intensive Interaction is new to the professionals you are involved with, you can point them to information about it (see Chapter 11) so that they can explore the big picture and see what training opportunities exist. However, if you want them to start using it with your child, the most powerful message is going to be your own story, and the evidence of progress and greater inclusion that Intensive Interaction is bringing about for your child.

Record-keeping in the family

As parents we are trying to have as ordinary a life as possible with our families. We have chosen to use Intensive Interaction with our children so that we can enjoy a closer relationship with them and enhance the quality of their lives. We are going to be excited about the progress our child makes, but in a family context we are not going to be prioritising writing notes or shooting video to record it. If you have time, and only if you do, shooting some video and making informal notes every now and again can give invaluable evidence of progress to other people. If you have been on one of Dave Hewett's training days you will know what a strong impact video can have. A series of short clips can speak volumes about doing Intensive Interaction, as well as track progress.

If you can, shoot some baseline video of your child on their own before you start Intensive Interaction with them. I aim to take some video once or twice a term; you need to work out what is realistic for you. I also keep a file in the kitchen and jot down anything worth noting under the date. Keep the notes brief and factual and try to note new things that happen. Jotting down notes and taking video are also a good way to stimulate reflection on what has been going on, what is working well and what you might do differently in future.

Have a look at Chapter 7 if you would like more advice on record-keeping and shooting video. Enlisting the help of a friend or family member to take the video can work well, especially if they are into technology and can save you time by putting it onto DVD too. Above all, keep a sense of perspective about it and do not get stressed if it is all too much.

Other people are often open to new ideas and ways of working but this is not always the case. If people or services providing support to you and your child are not interested, try to maintain a positive relationship with them. Be polite but assertive and persistent. Keep talking about the benefits of Intensive Interaction for your child at meetings, with video and written evidence if possible.

Parents in a 'community of practice'

It is very different doing Intensive Interaction at home, say, to doing it in a school or residential setting alongside other staff. If you were doing it as part of your job, you might get more informal and formal opportunities to reflect on your practice, share ideas and get further training. Even if other family members and others involved with the family take on and use the approach, it is usually the parents who have initiated its use who continue to be the driving force, who are the informal trainers, advice-givers and organisers. It is good for us to meet people using Intensive Interaction in other places, either other parents or professionals. It is helpful to share experiences, ask for and give advice and learn more. Chapter 11 gives you information on ways you can link in with other Intensive Interaction practitioners.

You can also build your own network of support informally at home, sharing ideas and reflecting on practice with other people who use the approach or similar interactive approaches with your child. In my case I chat about George, my son, with my husband, paid workers who help out, volunteers who give us respite, and a music therapist who comes to the house.

When I think about George's 'circle of support', the people who care about him and are his friends, they are all people who have built their relationship with him through Intensive Interaction. That is how they know who he is, what he likes to do, where he likes to go and what makes him laugh. He is 13 now, and as I look to his future, ensuring people who work with him know about and use Intensive Interaction becomes a priority, to ensure that his quality of life continues to be enhanced by relationships like these.

Part 3

Issues, topics and community

10

Some associated issues and topics

Dave Hewett

This chapter looks at:

- **'Age-appropriateness' and developmental appropriateness**
- **Physical contact**
- **Use of video recordings**
- **Challenging behaviours.**

'Age-appropriateness' and developmental appropriateness

In our field of work, for many years now, there has been a fashion for employing a notion of what has been termed 'age-appropriateness'. In its crudest form, it seems to be a viewpoint that is something like this:

'People who have severe learning difficulties should only have experiences in line with their chronological ages.'

There is no doubt that the managers and practitioners who have this viewpoint and operate practices arising from it have in mind a laudable motive such as the giving of esteem and respect to a socially disadvantaged person.

However, the result has often been what we and many others view as severe consequences for people who have severe learning difficulties. Occurrences such as adult voting citizens having their personal possessions taken away from them, staff refusing to give regard to their expressed desires or wishes, staff failing to communicate with a person in a way she or he can understand, staff refusing to give comfort and reassurance to a person, refusing in any way to play with a person, basically refusing to acknowledge the inner person, and so on.

Intensive Interaction seems to have had a positive influence on the thinking around this issue. There seems to be increasing realisation about, and acceptance of, the reality that where the person is developmentally 'at' is the critical issue, more than their chronological age. In the name of 'age-appropriateness' a service can consistently fail to give any regard to the developmental reality of the inner person. This does not make sense. This is particularly the case with communication work. If communication routines are not developmentally pertinent to the person, they do not take place.

It is interesting to do a little research in order to read all the background literature and research on age-appropriateness (AA); there is a surprising and interesting result:

- I can find little, well, next to no literature on this topic in the literature of our field.

- The topic is not addressed in the 'big' books on SLD and autism and SLD curriculum by the famous people. This is the case when some of these writers are nonetheless avowed age-appropriateness enthusiasts.

- I can find no reference to AA in the Office for Standards in Education (OFSTED) protocol. I assume that when inspectors make criticisms on AA grounds, it is a personal preference.

- Likewise the above to the social care inspectorate.

- Age-appropriateness is *not* an aspect of normalisation philosophy or theorising. Quite the contrary, the original theorists like Nirje were taken aback by efforts to make people with learning disabilities appear normal. Nirje and others insisted that normalisation was about making normalising experiences *available*, not about operating a concept of normal.

 A suggestion for a statement on age-appropriateness which can be included in a policy or guideline document supporting staff practice

In daily working practices and documentation of practice, it is important to have working practices that give regard to the person's chronological age and status as an adult voting citizen. Wherever possible, bearing in mind the ability and understanding of the person, these practices should also promote the awareness and understanding of her or himself as an adult voting citizen.

However, at the same time and without any sense of contradiction or paradox, members of staff should also be offering practices and activities which give regard to where the person is at cognitively, psychologically, emotionally and communicatively. To fail to do this is to fail to give regard to, and make contact with, the true, inner person.

Achieving the above may seem like, and can be, a complicated operation. It implies a sense of balance and differentiation in the way in which members of staff view the person and offer activities and experiences. Activities and experiences may need to be balanced throughout the day with various activities geared towards certain aspects of the person, and other activities addressing

> other aspects. Often it will be possible to promote activities and experiences which address all aspects simultaneously.
>
> In achieving this sense of balance across the spread of activities for the person, it is important to remember that there will be a different set of balances for each individual person.

- I think there is some anecdotal evidence (literally, things I have heard said, not written) that with people with high-ability learning difficulties, it is life-enhancing for them and their self-image if those of us around them treat them according to their chronological age. This seems logical. However, there are still, I believe, huge issues for the more able around the developmental experiences, particularly play, that they do not receive or have facilitated. Even with the 'more able', where are they actually 'at' cognitively, psychologically, emotionally?

- It seems therefore that age-appropriateness is actually a vague notion that has gained some sort of influence and popularity through a sort of 'politically correct' repetition. It has no proper foundation. It is not supported in our literature, it has not been inquired into nor researched; a definition or a philosophy has never been elaborated in a learned fashion.

- This is not to suggest that every single tiny thing that we do in our practices should be evidence based and/or supported by research/inquiry. This is a clearly untenable position that disavows staff common-sense and working from general experience. However, the notion of AA has been pervasively influential for so many years (particularly significantly in adult services) with so many far-reaching and fundamental effects on the lives of service users. In this case, it is absolutely imperative, indeed ethically a given, that the practices that arise should be psychologically and philosophically substantiated by literature in refereed publications. This has not been done.

- I have never, ever, anywhere seen a (written) *policy* on AA. In adult services particularly, it seems necessary to cover everything, all practices with a policy. But not age-appropriateness. I think it is an interesting exercise to demand that an age-appropriateness enthusiast should write such a policy.

- When practitioners use the term 'age-appropriateness', I feel they do it rather airily, believing they are referring to a well-known and properly established working concept, unknowing of the reality.

Physical contact

Some years ago, in our field of work with people who have SLD, it seemed as though our general sense of anxiety about abuse and protection was causing a drift towards absolute 'no touch' policies. That trend seems to be lessening at the time of writing. Just as with age-appropriateness, over recent years, the existence of Intensive Interaction seems to have played a positive part in any debate about this issue.

Those of us who work on Intensive Interaction have always recognised and endorsed the need for proper protection procedures for pupils, service users and indeed for staff. There are obvious real concerns around such as:

- inadvertently stimulating sexual arousal with physically mature people

- your intentions being misinterpreted by an observer, accusations of abuse

- the whole thing gets out of hand, the person becomes 'clingy'

- use of physical contact contributes to an excess of emotional bonding.

The potential problems outlined above need to be borne in mind and, sometimes, addressed. Those of us writing here recognise fully that to touch, or not to touch, is not a simple issue that can be resolved in any simple way.

However, we have also maintained that the people we are supporting can want and need simple human contact for a variety of absolutely ordinary human and developmental reasons. Individual members of staff and teams working together will always be presented with the complications of the people they are supporting and the need to respond thoughtfully to each individual person.

This human reality has recently been recognised by child protection bodies who have become concerned that their right and proper work on child protection, may nonetheless contribute also to a general atmosphere of anxiety where many parents are no longer touching and nurturing their children properly or sufficiently. (See 'Rationale', box.)

The worst-case scenario would be a prevalence of 'no touch' rules. This we feel would be a disaster. It would be a personal disaster for each individual adult or child who is still at a very early stage of development – psychologically, emotionally or communicatively. But we suggest it would be a disaster, too, for our field and even our society – our approach to dealing with human complexity would be to institutionally ignore it.

 Rationale

Touch is essential in order to provide sensitive and good quality care for the children and young people we support. Used in context and with empathy, touch supports the development of our natural interactions with the children and young people we care for.

Staff often have concerns and fears about the use of touch for various reasons. This policy sets out to clarify the reasons and conditions for touch.

(From 'Specimen Policy on Touch' available from The Intensive Interaction website – www.intensiveinteraction.co.uk – 'Downloadable Resources'.)

Once again, when you study the literature of our work for guidance on physical contact issues, it is nothing short of scandalous how little has been produced. There has been little general learned debate in our field, there are few journal articles, and it is not really addressed in the 'big' books on our work. There still seems to be a reluctance in many services to provide proper, positive guidance to staff on these issues. What literature there is has mostly been produced by writers on Intensive Interaction and there is a small, growing body of it (see 'Further reading' at the end of the chapter).

So, let us get positive. What can we actively do on this issue? Here are suggestions:

- Be aware at all times in your practice of the need to be careful, to give regard to the difficulties, the guidelines and so on, but also be human.

- Talk about it. Make it a topic of ordinary human discussion among your team and with your managers. Do not allow this to be the great 'unmentionable' issue.

- Do some reading to support those discussions.

- Talk with the team and managers about the need for guidelines for safeguarding and for positively providing this aspect of meaningful human interaction. (See for example 'Suggestions for guidelines for safeguards' below.)

- Write the guidelines or borrow some already written ones and then work to keep them as a living, working document in your workplace.

- If anybody tells you there is a 'no touch' policy, ask to see the policy. A 'policy' is only a policy if it is written down. If it is not written down, it is just somebody's viewpoint.

 Suggestions for guidelines for safeguards

- **Know why you do it**. Be knowledgeable on the purposes of using physical contact by discussion, thought and by reading the pertinent psychological and developmental literature.
- **Have consent from the person**. Obey the usual conventions concerning making physical contact with another person. If you rarely get consent to touch, then go back a few stages and work toward obtaining willingly given consent. At the very least, physical contact may be necessary to carry out basic care.
- **Be prepared to discuss and explain your practices**. First and foremost by being knowledgeable, as above.
- **Document – have it acknowledged in the school curriculum document or work-place brochure**. The culture and working practices of the school or other work place are acknowledged in the curriculum document or work-place brochure and this will include explication of the use of physical contact and the purposes of it.

(Continued)

(Continued)

- **Document – have it acknowledged in any individual programme for the person**. Be assertive. If you are certain that use of physical content is fulfilling the person's needs educationally or developmentally, then state this in the documentation drawn up to support work with that person.
- **Have good teamwork, both organisational and emotional**. Teamworking practices should literally facilitate staff working together in teams so that staff or students are rarely alone. The teamworking ethos should also include good discussions among staff concerning the emotional aspects of the work, including crucially, orientations toward the issue of the use of physical contact.
- **Use of physical contact should be discussed openly and regularly**. There should be no sense of furtiveness or 'hidden curriculum'. This important aspect of teaching technique should tangibly be a matter of open discussion and study.
- **Have others present where possible**. The most basic safeguard for staff and students is to have other staff present in the room when in situations where physical contact is likely to be used.

Use of video recordings

There can be reluctance to use video within some services. We have encountered services where no video recordings or even still photographs may be taken of people who cannot expressly give their consent in speech. This seems somewhat extreme. We know of no services who do not take their service users out and about in the community, even though there are video cameras recording us everywhere.

Sometimes this reluctance is placed within an interpretation of protecting vulnerable adults policies, though video is not specifically mentioned in the protection of vulnerable adults (POVA) legislation and national guidelines.

We suggest that use of video in enhancing communication work with a person is demonstrably and self-evidently in a person's best interests. In the same way we universally judge that holding meetings about them and keeping written records on them without their expressed consent, is in their best interests.

Nonetheless, we do not in any way suggest that each member of staff and service should not treat this issue with appropriate responsibility and propriety. We do suggest you follow the brief guidance offered below:

- Ask to see the written policy and guidelines of your service.

- If the service does not have written procedures or guidelines, suggest working together to write them.

- Make sure that you follow the proper procedures in the guidelines.

- Make sure that you observe data protection rules:

- Video data stored secure under lock and key (never taken home).
- Only kept for the period of time that it is clearly necessary to see it.
- Viewing of the video restricted to those persons who have a clear and definable 'need to view' which is in the best interests of the service user.

- Never, never use your mobile phone video function (your phone should never be turned on during working hours).

Most of the early research that gave us the understandings of the beautiful intricacies of parent–infant interactions took place using analysis of video recordings. All the research and development work on Intensive Interaction took place using analysis of video recordings. Used well and properly, use of video has the potential to greatly enhance the quality of life of each person we are working for.

Challenging behaviours

There are two main questions about challenging behaviours that usually crop up. We briefly address each in turn:

1. How do you do Intensive Interaction with people liable to be challenging or even violent? Well, carefully mostly. It must be clear that the activities are usually occurring with two people in close proximity, frequently making physical contact even. But this is not a given. It is not essential to be close to the person. Intensive Interaction has frequently been commenced with someone with the member of staff several metres away, even on the other side of the room. Of course, you look to establish the exchange, some turn-taking using visual and auditory channels.

    Over time, as the participants grow in confidence and the activities are enjoyably established, it is of course possible to start being closer together, even ultimately touching. Even so, most staff working in such circumstances report that somewhere along the line you can make a mistake and receive the consequences.

    The original development work on Intensive Interaction took place with adult people living in a large long-stay hospital. Many of them were people who were capable of the most severe challenging behaviour. Some of them were sectioned under the mental health act due to their potential for difficult behaviour. The staff working with them felt that Intensive Interaction and the general 'way of being' that came with it was easily the most effective way of working with those students.

    Furthermore, they frequently commented that they felt more secure. Due to the sensitive nature of the 'tuning-in' that they learnt in order to carry our Intensive Interaction, they felt that they could 'read' their people much more easily, knew them in more depth, and could more easily anticipate the changing flow of their moods and behaviour.

2. Does Intensive Interaction have a beneficial effect on a person's challenging behaviour? Yes, pretty much always. One reason is because there are many

senses in which behaviour difficulties are communication difficulties. If you enhance a person's abilities to communicate and relate better – at however basic a level – there is likely to be a corresponding beneficial pay-off in that person's behaviour. Actually that's fairly true for all of us. Let us break that down into a short list of likely reasons:

(a) Communication frustrations are reduced.
(b) The person has the benefits of a general sense of connection with others and literally being able to connect frequently.
(c) Many behaviour difficulties are likely to be effective negative interactions from a person who has little ability for positive interactions.
(d) Effective communication enhances self-esteem and other aspects of well-being.
(e) Likewise for the deep benefits likely to occur from being able to have and take part in relationships.

Further reading 📖

Forster, S. (2010) 'Age-appropriateness: enabler or barrier to a good life for people with profound intellectual and multiple disabilities?', *Journal of Intellectual and Developmental Disability*, 35(2): 129–31.

Nind, M. and Hewett, D. (1996) 'When age-appropriateness isn't appropriate', in J. Coupe-O'Kane and J. Goldbart (eds), *Whose Choice?* London: David Fulton.

There are sections on AA in:

Nind, M. and Hewett, D. (2001) *A Practical Guide to Intensive Interaction*. Kidderminster: British Institute of Learning Disabilities.

Nind, M. and Hewett, D. (2005) *Access to Communication: Developing the Basics of Communication with People with Severe Learning Difficulties through Intensive Interaction*. 2nd edn. London: David Fulton. (1st edn, 1994.)

Publications about physical contact in the field of learning difficulty and ASD:

Hewett, D. (2007) 'Do touch: physical contact and people who have severe, profound and multiple learning difficulties', *Support for Learning*, 22(3): 116–23.

Hewett, D. (2008) 'Do touch', *Caring*, Summer: 16–19. (Churches' Child Protection Advisory Service.)

'"No" to arm's length – Yes to good sense!' *Caring*, Summer: 16–19. (Churches' Child Protection Advisory Service.)

Rhodes, J. and Hewett, D. (2010) 'The human touch: physical contact and making a social world available for the most profoundly disabled'. *PMLD Link*, 22(2): 11–14.

There are sections on physical contact issues in:

Nind, M. and Hewett, D. (2001) *A Practical Guide to Intensive Interaction*. Kidderminster: British Institute of Learning Disabilities.

Nind, M. and Hewett, D. (2005) *Access to Communication: Developing the Basics of Communication with People with Severe Learning Difficulties through Intensive Interaction*. 2nd edn. London: David Fulton. (1st edn, 1994.)

There are many references in:

Firth, G. and Barber, M. (2011) *Using Intensive Interaction with a Person with a Social or Communication Impairment.* London: Jessica Kingsley.

Nind, M. (2009) 'Promoting the emotional well-being of people with profound and multiple intellectual disabilities; a holistic approach through Intensive Interaction', in J. Pawlyn and S. Carnaby (eds), *Profound Intellectual and Multiple Disabilities: Nursing Complex Needs.* Chichester: Wiley-Blackwell.

Zeedyk, M. (ed.) (2008) *Promoting Social Interaction for Individuals with Communicative Impairments.* London: Jessica Kingsley.

Two excellent, readable volumes overviewing general physical contact issues and research:

Field, T. (2001) *Touch.* Cambridge, MA: MIT Press.

Montague, A. (1986) *Touching: The Human Significance of the Skin.* New York: Harper and Row.

11

The Intensive Interaction community

Graham Firth

This chapter looks at:

- **The Intensive Interaction 'Community of Practice'**
- **The Intensive Interaction Institute**
- **The Intensive Interaction newsletters**
- **The Intensive Interaction Regional Support Groups**
- **Intensive Interaction on the World Wide Web.**

The Intensive Interaction 'Community of Practice'

We have long felt that the best way to 'do' Intensive Interaction is to do it with the support and encouragement of a group of concerned and sympathetic people. It is even better if these people also share the same perspective and the same goals. Such a group of people might be described as a 'Community of Practice'.

 A 'Community of Practice' (or 'CoP' for short) is a special group of people 'who share a concern, a set of problems, or a passion about a topic, and who deepen their understanding and knowledge of this area by interacting on an on-going basis' (Wenger, 1998: 4).

For individual Intensive Interaction practitioners, getting together to form a group that acts like an Intensive Interaction 'community of practice' (see the 'What is a community of practice?' for a description) can be extremely helpful. Such a group of people can be very supportive as they will collectively understand the ups (and on occasions the downs) of working in this way.

What is a 'Community of Practice'?

- A 'Community of Practice' is a group of people who share an interest or passion about a particular issue or way of working.
- A 'Community of Practice' is a group of people who work together in a supportive and practical way.
- A 'Community of Practice' is a group of people who continuously look to develop the skills and knowledge that they share.
- A 'Community of Practice' is a supportive network of people that is also accessible to newcomers or 'novice practitioners' that is, people who initially know very little about the shared 'CoP' issue or way of working.
- A 'Community of Practice' is a group of people who help 'novice practitioners' develop their understanding of the 'CoP' issue and way of working, and this is allowed to happen at whatever pace and to whatever extent is appropriate and achievable.

Such an Intensive Interaction 'CoP' can act as a non-judgemental sounding-board for people to discuss and jointly reflect on any difficulties associated with using Intensive Interaction. Equally, they can also be a group of people with whom to share any achievements and successes – a very important process.

Having access to such a supportive 'CoP' network also allows practitioners to seek advice from more experienced and knowledgeable Intensive Interaction 'old-timers' ('old-timers' being people who have used Intensive Interaction for longer – they are not necessarily older in years). Such Intensive Interaction 'old-timers' are useful people to have around as they will have encountered and worked through a broad range of Intensive Interaction issues and experiences.

Such an Intensive Interaction 'CoP' should also help individual practitioners share out any feelings of personal responsibility for the success, or otherwise, of introducing and supporting an Intensive Interaction intervention. The benefits of this feeling of shared responsibility should not be underestimated, as feeling personally responsible for an Intensive Interaction intervention can sometimes seem burdensome.

This process of 'CoP' community support should also be a two-way process, with all the members of any 'CoP' benefiting from the assistance of the other members – being part of the community is as much about giving support (which has its own beneficial effects) as it is about receiving it – which is self-evidently a good thing.

The help of a supportive Intensive Interaction 'CoP' can also be very useful because, at times outside of actually doing any Intensive Interaction, there is still a lot of important work to do. This might be when practitioners:

- spend time together reflecting on their current work with an individual, for example, by talking together about their own Intensive Interaction work or watching and reflecting on a video record of themselves or other practitioners using Intensive Interaction with a particular person, or

- when people work together to develop a better understanding of the approach, for example, by reading and discussing Intensive Interaction books, newsletter articles or research papers, or

- when people look to improve their own skills in practically applying Intensive Interaction, for example, by watching and discussing a video of other people doing Intensive Interaction – possibly including some of the published training videos featuring experienced Intensive Interaction practitioners.

These are all things best achieved with the active help and support of encouraging, well-informed and understanding fellow practitioners.

The way a 'Community of Practice' works tends to be different from some other ways that people share skills and knowledge between themselves, and thus eventually make 'experts' from people who start out as novices in some particular area of learning.

In some more formal ways of developing a person's expertise, a relatively small number of currently recognised 'experts' decide who else should also be allowed to become an expert, and when and how such a person might be allowed to do this.

Often, such formal 'expert' ways of working tend to develop into hierarchies, and the 'expert' people at the top of the hierarchy tend to have the power to make judgements on everyone else's ability and whether or not they can participate in certain activities.

Thus more formal 'experts' can, and often do decide exactly what should be done, and also who should be allowed to do certain things (and who should *not* be allowed to do certain things).

Generally an Intensive Interaction 'Community of Practice' will be a supportive group of people who share the necessary knowledge and skills associated with Intensive Interaction. However, in reality it should be acknowledged that the levels of Intensive Interaction skill and knowledge may well vary among a group's membership (some people being more knowledgeable and experienced 'old-timers' and some people being more 'novices'). However, whatever the levels of our own Intensive Interaction experience and knowledge, all of us can learn more, and we tend to learn best collectively by helping each other.

As a 'CoP' is generally seen as an informally structured group of people, it is important that they should always remain open and inviting to newcomers or 'novice' practitioners. Such potentially inexpert 'novices' should then be supported to gradually take on the basic skills and develop the required knowledge to practice Intensive Interaction in increasingly competent and confident ways, and this should happen at the pace and to the degree that is appropriate for them.

A 'Community of Practice' has been defined as consisting of three distinct aspects: 'mutual engagement', 'joint enterprise' and 'shared repertoire' (Wenger, 1998: 72–3):

1. **Mutual engagement**: through participation in the 'CoP', individual members build relationships that bind the group together as a social entity.
2. **Joint enterprise**: through a process of continuous discussion and clarification, members of the 'CoP' build a shared understanding of the issue(s) that bind them together.
3. **Shared repertoire**: in the pursuit of their joint enterprise the 'CoP' collectively develops a set of shared practices or ways of working.

Thus such a 'CoP' process enables the development of a greater shared understanding of the relevant 'CoP' issues, where shared experiences and knowledge of the 'CoP' 'joint enterprise' (that is Intensive Interaction) are more easily communicated and understood by the community's members. Within any Intensive Interaction 'CoP' a 'shared repertoire' (see above) can then be developed among the group's members by sharing any individually relevant knowledge and Intensive Interaction experiences, for example, by jointly viewing, discussing and collectively analysing Intensive Interaction sessions, either live or on video.

Intensive Interaction 'CoP's can be practically developed or accessed in a number of ways, such as:

- by attending a local Intensive Interaction Regional Support Group (see later for details), or

- by being developed within individual organisations (for example, within a school or residential service), or

- by being mutually developed across a number of services (for example, by being organised by staff or carers across a number of schools or residential services), or

- by building an Intensive Interaction community around an individual who will benefit from the approach (this process being similar to the creation of a circle of friendship).

It should be acknowledged that, within any 'CoP', members are not only responsible for the further development of their own skills and knowledge – they also have a role to play in supporting others to develop their practices and knowledge. Then as new or novice members' Intensive Interaction skills and knowledge develop they are then enabled to contribute to the shared understanding of the group. Thus within any 'CoP' there should be an identifiable upward spiral (that looks and sounds familiar!) of shared Intensive Interaction knowledge and practical skills.

An Intensive Interaction 'CoP' should always remain an open, lively and active group of people, a community that will be strengthened by the arrival of new people – it will be such people (the novices) who will eventually share the responsibility for further developing the Intensive Interaction 'CoP'. New people might also, if welcomed and supported, bring new insights and new skills to the group (for example new skills and understanding of the latest technology, for example, computer editing of video). They will also become tomorrow's experienced and knowledgeable 'old-timers' (again no ageism meant or implied). After all, they are the future of Intensive Interaction!

In summary therefore:

- A 'Community of Practice' should be seen as helpful because:

  - in an Intensive Interaction 'CoP' the more experienced Intensive Interaction practitioners can help to support the development of the more 'novice' Intensive Interaction practitioners

  - in an Intensive Interaction 'CoP' all the members can help each other to develop their combined Intensive Interaction skills and understanding, and

  - in an Intensive Interaction 'CoP' members can help bring new skills and insights to Intensive Interaction more generally, for example, through collaborative discussion or study.

- Therefore members of an Intensive Interaction 'Community of Practice' all have an important and active role to play – they should be supportive of fellow practitioners and help with the general advancement and development of Intensive Interaction.

The Intensive Interaction Institute

First suggested at the 2006 UK Intensive Interaction Conference in Leeds as a realistic and desirable concept (and over five years spent in various stages of fermentation) the formation of the Intensive Interaction Institute finally came to fruition as a not-for-profit company registered in 2011. The Intensive Interaction Institute was identified by its founding members as a central vehicle to continue the process of Intensive Interaction definition, dissemination and development.

Initially consisting of 'board members' Dave Hewett, Cath Irvine and Graham Firth (joined by Isle of Man clinical lead speech and language therapist, Jan Gordon, in 2009 and company secretary, Sarah Forde, in early 2011) the institute came into being after an extended, and at times seemingly tortuous process of consultation and development work that included collecting the views and advice of many supportive and helpful people.

From the earliest times, and initially with the help of clinical psychologist Dr Peter Coia, the aims of the Intensive Interaction Institute were formulated as:

- defining the nature and characteristics of Intensive Interaction

- developing the theory and practice of Intensive Interaction

- disseminating further awareness, knowledge, and understanding of Intensive Interaction

- fostering and delivering high-quality training in the theory and practices of Intensive Interaction.

Despite the surprisingly extended period required to organise the institute's establishment (significantly speeded up in the later stages by the help of astute and businesslike company secretary, Sarah Forde), during the initial set-up phase significant preparation work was undertaken to support the creation of a range of Intensive Interaction learning resources, including:

- An expanded www.intensiveinteraction.co.uk website (initially created, administered and funded by Dave Hewett), that increasingly features a collection of useful Intensive Interaction resources, information, news, articles and past copies of the *Intensive Interaction Newsletter*. This site also lists contact details of the burgeoning UK Intensive Interaction Regional Support Groups (RSGs), and dates for upcoming meetings of these RSGs.

- The Intensive Interaction Assessed Practitioner course (chiefly written by board member Cath Irvine, and trialled and developed with the help of many student Intensive Interaction coordinators) which is an extremely comprehensive distance learning pack designed to develop individual Intensive Interaction practice and reflectivity.

- The Intensive Interaction Induction and Information Packs (created in association with the Leeds Partnerships NHS Trust), designed to support information dissemination to particular groups of people (for example, care staff, parents and support staff) who are unfamiliar with the approach.

The Intensive Interaction Institute board became, and remains, centrally involved in the organisation of the annual Intensive Interaction conferences in the UK, helping define the particular focus and structure of each year's conferences.

One of the roles taken on by the Intensive Interaction Institute is to act as an official Intensive Interaction archivist, and thus to be a central body that acts as a central repository of relevant Intensive Interaction research papers and articles (both published and unpublished). The aim of this archive work is to create a comprehensive Intensive Interaction library for anyone engaged in an Intensive Interaction associated programme of study to access any potentially relevant Intensive Interaction material.

The Intensive Interaction newsletters

First published in 2003 by the Learning Disability Psychology Services of the Leeds Partnerships NHS Trust the UK *Intensive Interaction Newsletter* is available free of charge (via email) and is released on a quarterly basis.

Purposely positive and supportive of Intensive Interaction practitioners and advocates, the newsletter is available from the official Intensive Interaction website at http://www.intensiveinteraction.co.uk/blog/leeds-ii-newsletters/ or at the Leeds Partnerships NHS Trust website at http://www.leedspft.nhs.uk/our_services/ld/ intensiveinteraction.

Figure 11.1   The *Intensive Interaction Newsletter* issue 35

The newsletter is compiled with the following specifications in mind:

- That the content is varied and of interest to a broad readership (that is from multidisciplinary groupings, deliberately including parents, carers and various professional groups).

- That the content is aimed at a readership that works with people of all age groups – early years, schools, children's services, adult services and older adult services.

- That jargonistic and over-academic language is avoided whenever possible to make the newsletter content accessible to the varied readership.

- That the newsletter actively sets out to attract contributions from current Intensive Interaction practitioners, that is, the diffuse and multidisciplinary 'Community of Intensive Interaction Practitioners'.

- That the newsletter reflects the general views and aspirations of the Intensive Interaction Institute.

The content of the newsletter generally includes:

➢ general Intensive Interaction news
➢ Intensive Interaction research reviews and summaries
➢ details of new Intensive Interaction resources e.g. books and DVDs etc.
➢ details of upcoming Intensive Interaction conferences
➢ details of Intensive Interaction training opportunities
➢ individual Intensive Interaction practitioner accounts
➢ details for the Intensive Interaction Regional Support Groups and much more (sometimes)

Figure 11.2 Newsletter content

The Intensive Interaction Regional Support Groups

An initial wish of the Intensive Interaction Institute board was to create the possibility for individual practitioners to access supportive Intensive Interaction communities, and this came to fruition in the shape of the UK Intensive Interaction Regional Support Groups. After prolonged discussion between a number of Intensive Interaction practitioners, the idea of introducing some structure and standards into the dissemination and support of the approach was identified as desirable. Also, it was acknowledged that, for a number of reasons, Intensive Interaction might be taken more seriously by services and organisations if there was an established and visible means of external support available in the locality.

 What are Regional Support Groups for?

- Supporting current Intensive Interaction practitioners, for example, by sharing and discussing case studies/video footage and collectively reflecting on good Intensive Interaction practice.

- Supporting and encouraging novice practitioners, for example, parents, by providing a shared and supportive learning environment.

- Disseminating Intensive Interaction knowledge and information, for example, about conferences, practice guidelines, new books and DVDs, training opportunities, and so on.

- Providing opportunities for peer support, problem solving and celebrations of success.

(Continued)

(Continued)

- Emphasising and furthering the multidisciplinary nature of Intensive Interaction work and providing a place for productive networking.
- Being a link to and from the Intensive Interaction Institute.
- Participating in relevant studies/questionnaires when requested by others researching the use of Intensive Interaction.

Central to the idea of creating accessible Intensive Interaction 'Communities of Practice', the UK Regional Support Groups were formalised to provide a friendly and encouraging forum for Intensive Interaction focused discussion and collaborative learning. Some of the groups had already been meeting as professional Special Interest Groups (SIGs), but some of these groups then joined the national network once it was officially announced by Cath Irvine at the 2008 Intensive Interaction conference in Birmingham.

Generally meeting every three months, each group is seen as semi-autonomous and democratic in nature. The groups are run by the membership specifically for the benefit of the group's members. Although there is usually a basic agenda, the content and structure of each meeting is decided upon by mutual agreement to address any specific issues arising for those people who attend.

Sometimes RSG meetings are arranged around a particular theme or a special presentation, and in the past these have included:

- looking at the latest Intensive Interaction information or training resources, for example, the newest DVDs and latest Intensive Interaction books

- an 'introductory' presentation for parents – setting out the basics of Intensive Interaction for parents who might not have heard of the approach, or currently have little understanding of the rationale or techniques used

- video analysis for Intensive Interaction – how to structure collective video analysis most productively

- record-keeping and analysis to highlight progress in Intensive Interaction.

Responsibility for organising the groups can be relatively fluid, although there is often a dedicated individual or small group at the centre of each RSG that acts as a contact and organises the venues (and refreshments, if there are any).

The latest contact details for each Intensive Interaction Regional Support Group can be found at http://www.intensiveinteraction.co.uk/regional-networks/ and the latest information on the dates and venues of any upcoming RSG meetings can generally be found on the webpage.

 In early 2010 the first annual meeting for representatives of all the UK RSGs was held to provide a forum to support those individuals who voluntarily organise and facilitate the groups. This meeting was attended by representatives from Sunderland, Liverpool, Sheffield, Leeds, Macclesfield, London, Wales, Nottingham, Brighton and Oxford.

Thus the RSGs have now become part of the fabric of Intensive Interaction support and dissemination in those areas lucky enough to have them. Yet more new RSGs are being proposed and set up in other locations across the UK to help support, encourage and maintain the Intensive Interaction of many other dedicated practitioners.

Intensive Interaction on the World Wide Web

Many people nowadays find a significant amount of their initial information about Intensive Interaction through resources located via the Internet. Increasingly this will become a communication means that will significantly help to disseminate Intensive Interaction information and knowledge.

The current significant Intensive Interaction sites include:

www.IntensiveInteraction.co.uk – this is the 'official' Intensive Interaction website, and it contains various sections such as: About Intensive Interaction – with sections on 'Who is Intensive Interaction for?', 'The fundamentals of communication' and 'How does Intensive Interaction work?' There are also sections on publications on Intensive Interaction (with an extensive bibliography of Intensive Interaction research and papers), recommended books (with a list of the main Intensive Interaction books and others of associated interest); downloadable resources (with downloadable copies of the *Intensive Interaction Newsletter*, downloadable documents on touch guidelines and policies), details of the Regional Support Groups (with upcoming meetings and contact details), details of upcoming conferences, courses and events and a page with Intensive Interaction articles and 'blogs'.

http://www.leedspft.nhs.uk/our_services/ld/intensiveinteraction – the Leeds Partnerships NHS Trust's Intensive Interaction webpage includes a number of useful downloadable resources, which include: the most recent issue of the UK *Intensive Interaction Newsletter*; an 'Introduction to Intensive Interaction' pamphlet; an 'Intensive Interaction – Published Research Summaries Document' document; an 'Intensive Interaction published literature and information resources' document; a 'Framework for Recognising Attainment in Intensive Interaction' document; and a 'Strengths and Needs Analysis and Planning for Intensive Interaction' document.

 This site was acknowledged and recommended alongside www.Intensive Interaction.co.uk as the most useful site to access further Intensive Interaction resources and information in the UK government's learning disability policy document *Valuing People Now* (2009).

Intensive Interaction Users on Facebook. For those people who are Facebook users there is a dedicated page called 'Intensive Interaction Users' set up by Intensive Interaction Institute board member Cath Irvine. Go to www.facebook.com and search for Intensive Interaction Users. The site has a general 'wall' to post news, views or questions and receive comments or other contacts from fellow members. The Intensive Interaction Users site is used to share ideas, seek answers to particular problems and post relevant Intensive Interaction related information, and the page also has links to active discussion boards, Intensive Interaction related documents, Intensive Interaction Regional Support Group meeting details and updates, and (you have guessed it) much more.

www.bild.org.uk/pdfs/05faqs/ii.pdf – on the British Institute of Learning Disabilities (BILD) website there is a fact sheet on Intensive Interaction which can be downloaded as a pdf file (which are small and easy to email or store on a CD or memory stick). The fact sheet has sections on: 'Why Intensive Interaction?', 'What is Intensive Interaction?', 'When and where?' and 'who?'

http://en.wikipedia.org/wiki/Intensive_interaction – There is a page on Intensive Interaction on Wikipedia (the free Internet encyclopaedia). This page gives some information and also a bit of history and background on the approach, and some references to published papers are given. There are also embedded links within the text to help interested readers develop their understanding of associated issues and concepts.

References

Department of Health (2009) *Valuing People Now: A New Three-year Strategy for People with Learning Disabilities* available at www.dh.gov.uk/en/Publicationsandstatistics/Publications/Publications PolicyAndGuidance/DH_093377 accessed 15 January 2010.

Wenger, E. (1998) *Communities of Practice: Learning, Meaning, and Identity.* Cambridge: Cambridge University Press.

Bibliography

Specific texts are highlighted at the end of each chapter. The texts below provide more general overviews of all issues discussed.

Arnett, A. and Hewett, D. (1994) 'Safety first: violent and aggressive behaviour: principles for managing difficult situations', *Community Care,* 10 March.

Hewett, D. (ed.) (2011) *Intensive Interaction: Theoretical Perspectives.* London: Sage.

Nind, M. and Hewett, D. (1994) *Access to Communication: Developing the Basics of Communication with People with Severe Learning Difficulties through Intensive Interaction.* London: David Fulton.

Index

Added to a page number 'f' denotes a table.